LOVELY IS THE LEE

LOVELY IS THE LEE *by* ROBERT GIBBINGS

Engravings by the Author

New York · 1945

E · P · DUTTON & COMPANY, INC.

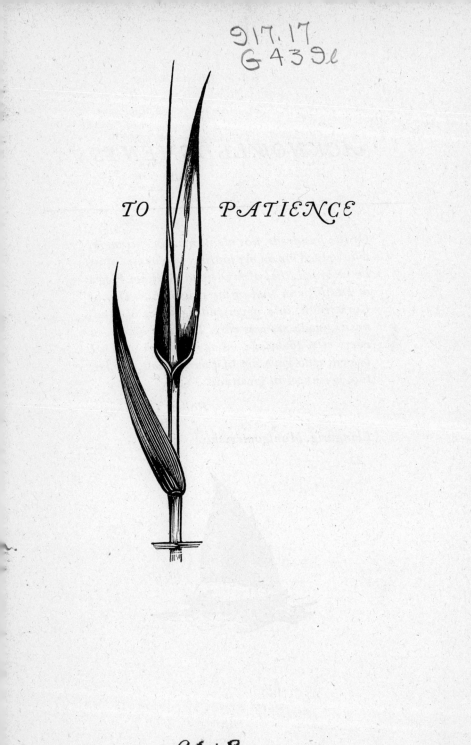

TO PATIENCE

ACKNOWLEDGMENTS

Of the hundreds, not mentioned in this book, who helped me on my journey two names must be recorded, that of my friend William Figgis of Dublin and that of my cousin Alec Day of Cork. Both, in a never-ending series of kindnesses, made my way easy. To those others, in every city, town and village through which I passed, who gave me of their richest, I offer, too, my sincerest gratitude.

Robert Gibbings

Llangurig, Montgomeryshire

LOVELY IS THE LEE

CHAPTER ONE

I WASN'T TEN MINUTES inside the door of the Royal Hotel at Galway before I was accosted on the stairs by a complete stranger, a young man of about thirty years of age.

'Come down till I treat you,' he said. As I turned to go with him he added: 'My name is Jimmy Dillon. What's yours?' I told him. 'I'll call you Bob,' he said.

We went down the stairs and into the bar. There were only two men there. One was small and wizened. He was wearing corduroy breeches and leggings, and was sitting before the fire, reading a newspaper. He took little notice of our entry. The other was heavily built and florid. He wore a mustard-coloured tweed suit, and overlapped a high stool beside the marble counter. His elbows rested on the counter and his chin was sunk in his fists. His lower lip was thrust far forward. He seemed to be weighed down with some great mental problem.

'You're someone,' he said, with emphasis, pointing his finger at me, as Jimmy and I came in. 'I seen you before.

I seen you at the station. You didn't see me. Your back was facing me. "That's a man," I said to Paddy Lydon, "that's a man," I said. My name is Laffin, Tim Laffin.' He swung round on his stool. The sunburnt dome of his bald head seemed to rise higher and higher above his ears. 'Now,' he said with great solemnity, 'I'm a plain man, a very plain man. I'm a man of few words. Tell me, in one sentence, in one sentence only, what's wrong with the world?'

It would not be the easiest question to answer in one sentence at any time, still less on the spur of the moment that one arrives in Galway. 'I suppose,' I ventured, 'the only hope is in a revival of real religion.'

'Isn't the Pope looking after that?' said the man at the fire.

'Shut up,' said the man of few words.

But I was punctured. Any great thoughts that I might have uttered were lost to the world.

Laffin began to speak again, but Jimmy interrupted him. Cattle were fetching five pounds more a head in England than in Ireland, he said.

'You'd get five pounds more for that glass of stout if you had it in hell,' said the man by the fire.

'You go to hell,' said Laffin.

'And send you my ashes as snuff. Wouldn't I laugh to see you sneezing!'

'Once that man's hat is on his head his house is thatched,' whispered Jimmy to me, pointing to the little man. 'He's a tangler. He hasn't the price of one beast in the world. But he's a good judge. He'll buy early, knowing he can sell at a profit before the day is out. He can't pay till he sells.'

The little man got up and left us.

'And he puts that many airs on him, looking down his

nose at every one,' added Jimmy a little louder, as the door closed.

'Them as looks down their nose don't see far beyond it,' said Laffin.

'And he's never in the same place two days—walks, walks, walks,' said Jimmy.

'Might as well tell a swallow not to travel,' said Laffin.

'Every man to his trade,' said Jimmy.

'There's a deal of difference between selling bad eggs and cooking them,' said Laffin. 'Now will ye all stop talking and listen to me for one moment!' he continued. 'One would think the lot of ye had been vaccinated with gramophone needles. Listen to me, now!'

But nobody would listen. The arrival of a party of drovers gave me an opportunity to slip away. Jimmy came after me. 'Will you come to the fair in the morning?' he asked. 'I'll call you at four o'clock.'

It was already getting dusk that evening as I wandered into the town. From the corners of narrow streets one caught glimpses of archways, and colour-washed walls lit by hidden lamps. There was no noise of traffic, except footsteps on the pavement. Groups of men stood at the corners of the streets, dark silhouettes of women in shawls passed by. One old woman coming round a corner nearly bumped into me. I stepped aside to let her pass. 'Wisha, God bless you,' she said as she went by.

Down by the Claddagh, the oldest fishing village in Ireland, I stopped to look over the bridge.

'You're a stranger here?' a man said to me.

'I am,' I answered.

'This is the Claddagh bridge,' he said, 'and the one above which you can't see in the dark is O'Brien's bridge, and the one above that is where you'll see the salmon waiting to go

over the weir, hundreds of them, thick as paving stones;
and in the summer as many visitors polishing the parapet
with their elbows, and gaping at the fish below who don't
give a damn for any of them.'

'D'you ever pick one out?' I asked.

'It's preserved,' he said.

'Even so?' I queried.

'Maybe,' he said with a smile.

After a pause while we watched the torrent of brown
flood water glinting in the light of the street lamps he spoke
again. 'There's the Spanish Arches behind you, but you
can't see them, and the Spanish Parade is alongside of
them. That's where you'd see the Spanish grandees in their
cocked hats walking out of a Sunday. How many hundred
years ago? I suppose it would be near five hundred. Galway
was a mighty fine place then.'

Again we watched the river sluicing down from Lough
Corrib.

'Have you been to the old jail,' he asked, 'with the skull
and the bones in stone over the door? Wasn't it the divil's
own thing for the judge to do, to condemn and hang his
own son?'

'But hadn't he committed a murder?'

'Yerra, murders were cheap enough in them days. Sure,
the whole world was murdering each other, same as they're
doing now indeed.'

'I believe,' I said, 'there are some who think that
Judge Lynch never did hang his son; that it's all a
story.'

'That he never hanged his son? Isn't it written up on the
wall with the year it happened, 1493, and all? And doesn't
the whole world know what lynch law means, and how
could it have spread the world if he never done it? I sup-

pose they'll say that Columbus never said mass in St. Nicholas beyond, before he went to America, and that he didn't take a Galway man with him, Rice de Culvey was his name. Faith, they'll say next that Columbus never discovered America at all.'

I thought it better not to hint that some thought America had been visited by the Portuguese at least fifty years earlier, and that there were Norse colonies in Greenland in the eleventh century.

'Come down with me now and I'll show you the Claddagh,' he said. 'Well, you can't see it; but we'll walk through it. 'Tis as well for you that you can't see it, for what is it now but slates and stones, and all the houses in straight lines. Planning, they calls that. There was a time when there were eight thousand in the Claddagh and they all fine healthy fishermen, and now there isn't five hundred. I tell you, the vests they wore in them days would make coats for men to-day. And they had their own king and queen, and not one of them would marry outside of the Claddagh, and they had their own wedding ring, the Claddagh ring, with the two hands catching hold of the crowned heart. And the houses were thatched, and warm in winter and cool in summer, and they didn't know what disease was, for no man died but by the will of God. And to-day, what with the damp out of the concrete floor under their feet, and the cold out of the slates over their heads, 'tis only one sneeze they need give and they drop dead.'

By this time we had reached the long pier that stretches out to the west of Galway Harbour. The moon was rising over the town, and the spire of the fourteenth-century church of St. Nicholas was silhouetted against the sky. Along the quays great, gaunt warehouses, with empty windows, told of former prosperity. Sea-gulls were crying out at sea. A man in a boat was singing *Galway Bay*.

> 'To see again the moonlight over Claddagh
> And to watch the sun go down on Galway Bay.'

'I'll see you back,' said my companion. We turned and walked through the narrow streets together. I could hear the notes of a harp from another street. At the hotel I invited him in.

'Oh, no!' he said, 'I never touch a drop.' Then as he was going: 'I'll leave some photos for you in the morning, and I'll see if I can find a ring.'

These Claddagh rings, of which my guide had spoken, have been for many generations the wedding token of the peasantry in the district stretching from the Aran Isles in the west through southern Connemara to some ten or twelve miles east of Galway. Although the device of two hands clasping a heart is not uncommon in many parts of Europe, the same with the crown added is extremely rare. It has, however, its counterpart in Spain, whence the design may have been brought to Galway by early traders. Similar rings in Brittany are handed down as heirlooms, as they are in Galway.

Like the better-known posy rings, an occasional one of these of Claddagh design had a motto inscribed on its inner surface. But a simple thought like 'Yours in hart,' such as we may find in Galway, scarcely compares with the more elaborate sentiments often found in the 'posies.' Nowhere in the west are we likely to come across such sophistication as

> 'Love him who gave thee this ring of gold,
> 'Tis he must kiss thee when thou 'rt old,'

or a line that offers such food for conjecture as

> 'Feare God, and lye abed till noone,'

or ambition like that of the bishop who, at his fourth wedding, had inscribed:

> 'If I survive I'll make thee five.'

Back in the hotel, in bed, I thought of the business man who had travelled with me that day from Dublin to Mullingar. He had just had to sack his foreman. 'The damn fellow kept on wanting to increase my profits. What the hell do I want more profits for? I have enough to live on. What I want is peace of mind and good fishing.' And there was the old woman who had been with me from Athlone to Athenry. She described the last moments of her husband. ' "I'm going now, Mary," he says, "and I'm very thankful to you, Mary," he says, "for all you have done for me; and when I see God I'll ask him to be good to you," he says. Them were his last words, and with that he shuts his eyes like a child, and goes straight to glory.'

CHAPTER TWO

IN THE BIG SQUARE, an hour before dawn, with no other light than that thrown from an occasional window and the one small lamp at each corner of the square, shadowy forms of men moved among shadowy forms of cattle. It had rained in the night, so that distorted reflections in the wet streets added to the weird shapes which formed and re-formed in the darkness.

There had been no need to call me. Animals under my window had kept me awake from an early hour. I met Jimmy by the weighbridge, at the far side of the square. He was after heifers, he told me. But just then he was buying a bullock. 'Come with me,' he said, when the deal was completed, as he headed up a road that led out of the town. His hope was to get in first with the farmers as they brought their stock from the country. Cattle were coming towards us in numbers, one moment steady and docile, the next twisting and turning, charging and slithering, rising on each other, then again running meekly under the shouts and blows of their drovers. In the darkness the black animals were almost invisible, and at times it needed considerable agility to avoid being impaled on their long horns. An occasional white beast shone luminous and ghostly. Sheep, in flocks, driven by boys with dogs, added to the confusion.

Jimmy seemed able to tell the age, sex, and quality of any and every beast by a mere prod of his fingers into its ribs. Now and again he would stop and ask an owner how much he wanted for a particular animal. Then a convulsion of argument would set in. Every offer was accompanied by a violent stroke of the fist into the open palm of the opposing party, an earnest of firm intentions.

Daylight was beginning to show when we got back to the square. It was now packed, packed thick, with animals, black Kerry cows, red and white shorthorns, bullocks and heifers, calves in high-penned, red-shafted donkey carts, an occasional bull.

'Did you know,' said Jimmy, 'that Kerrys are immune from T.B.? It's a pity they are no good for beef. A Kerry has never yet been known to carry tuberculosis, and they've tried to infect them.'

Standing about were elderly farmers in swallow-tailed coats and wide black hats, younger men in caps, mackintoshes, and leggings, old women in red petticoats, madonnas in shawls. Here and there an Aran islander in his distinctive dress of speckled blue and white homespun and sandals of rough hide—pampooties they call them.

On all sides bargains were being struck, and not only concerning cattle. When I went back to the hotel for breakfast two men were talking in the hall.

'What sort of a girl would she be?' asked one.

'A nice quiet little thing,' was the answer.

'And how many five-pound notes might she bring?'

'There'd be forty or fifty anyway.'

'I'll see what I can do,' said the first speaker.

'You ought to be ashamed of yourself, Paddy Muldoon,' said Miss McGovern, pushing her head through the open hatch from the bar. 'You ought to be ashamed of yourself, selling girls for money.'

'They get good homes,' said Paddy.

'Did *you* marry for the home, or for the woman?'

'Whisht a while, there's the man I'm wanting to see,' said Paddy, plunging his way through the crowd at the door.

The dining-room was full for breakfast. I shared a table with a man wearing a check coat and a yellow tie. 'I suppose you'll be coming to the races,' he said.

'I didn't know they were on,' I confessed.

'They're not on now,' he said, 'but they will be in July, the last week in July.'

'That's a good while ahead.'

'Oh, faith, if you don't book now you won't get a room. Book now,' he emphasized; 'it's the finest race meeting in the world. Galway goes mad. No one sleeps for a week.'

By early afternoon most of the business of the day was over. Jimmy was in bed asleep. My room being too near the front of the house for such composure I sought quiet beyond the Claddagh pier.

The tide was low and a dozen turnstones were busy on the shore. Here and there they ran, flicking aside the pebbles or the tufts of weed in search of unsuspecting victims. Gulls were there too, hoping to pounce on anything disclosed by the smaller birds, but gulls are clumsy on their feet and they seldom succeeded in their piratical intentions.

Like the redshank and many of the other small waders the turnstone on the wing is surprisingly unlike itself when on land. Indeed, it is often hard to believe that these unobtrusive little potterers of the shore can be the same birds that swing and swerve in crescent flight, their chevroned wings glinting like silver arrows.

Mergansers were there too. At one moment, in fast flight, they charged up the tide race, at the next, as urgently, they were dashing back to sea again. They formed into flocks, they separated into groups, they dived after fish, they flighted low over the water, they swung high over the docks.

In contrast to such hurry and bustle a red-throated diver swam sedately in the channel. Whereas the cormorant almost leaps out of the water before diving, and the merganser always seems in a hurry, the red-throated diver is essentially leisurely and dignified. When about to dive it merely puts its head below the surface and submerges. One is surprised to see that it has gone.

On some off-shore rocks a party of five oyster-catchers, with their black and white plumage fluffed out, stood like so many church dignitaries in their robes. Curlews were

there, too, probing deep with their long curved bills. Gulls
of varying maturity were there, the greater blackback in
the full glory of its adult plumage, the lesser blackback in
its third year, its beak still lacking the final gold and scarlet,
the herring gull in its second year's livery of mottled
brown. Men were gathering seaweed into carts. Women
were gathering periwinkles into buckets. Bodies of dead
green crabs lay among the tide ripples. No more anxiety
for them. Shells, too, of limpets, of whelks, of mussels, of
sea snails, of cockles, all gaping, empty; countless millions
of lives completed. As I returned a great northern diver
was swimming in the harbour, his mottled black and white
throat shimmering in the evening light. He who was bred
in Iceland or other far northern country must needs seek
his ration in Galway Bay. From the garbage dump beside
the pier decrepit humans were seeking the wherewithal of
their existence.

Back at the hotel, the promised photos were waiting for
me. There were several of trout being 'stripped' in the
hatchery, which now releases many hundreds of thousands
of trout fry into Lough Corrib each year. There were
others of catches of fish; trout averaging five or six pounds
each, taken from Lough Corrib. There was one of the only
public statue in Galway, that of Padraig O'Conaire, the
poet. There was one of the Galway fishing fleet, headed by
one of their own trawlers, with priests and acolytes on
board, sailing down Galway Bay to hold their annual
'Blessing of the Sea.' There was one of Ballynahinch Castle,
once the property of Richard Martin, M.P. 'Humanity
Martin' they called him. He was the promoter, in 1822, of
the first successful Bill for the protection of wild animals.
He was also one of the founders of the R.S.P.C.A.

Most poignant, the clear-cut features of Patrick Pearse,

with, on the back of the print, the lines he wrote on the eve
of his execution, Easter 1916.

'The beauty of the world hath made me sad,
This beauty that will pass;
Sometimes my heart hath shaken with great joy
To see a leaping squirrel in a tree,
Or a red ladybird upon a stalk,
Or little rabbits in a field at evening,
Lit by a slanting sun,
Or some green hill where shadows drifted by,
Some quiet hill where mountainy man hath sown
And soon would reap; near to the gate of Heaven;
Or children with bare feet upon the sands
Of some ebbed sea, or playing on the streets
Of little towns in Connacht,
Things young and happy.
And then my heart hath told me:
These will pass,
Will pass and change, will die and be no more,
Things bright and green, things young and happy;
And I have gone upon my way
Sorrowful.'

CHAPTER THREE

GALWAY IS A PLEASANT PLACE in which to do business. Soon after my arrival I called at the Munster and Leinster Bank to introduce myself. No, they hadn't had any advice note about me as yet, but if it was only a matter of money, there'd be no trouble about that. They had plenty of it. They'd be only too glad to accommodate me. They added that if I wanted a day's shooting or the loan of a car or a bicycle it would be equally simple. I went into the chemist's across the road from there and heard so much about trout that I forgot what I had gone in to buy. I collected my watch from a jeweller who had made some minor repairs to it. 'How much is that?' I asked. 'Yerra nothing at all.' I went into a stationer's to buy a few postcards. 'Can we send them for you?' I was asked.

I said to a man from over the border: 'It reminds me of Tir na n-Og, the land of the ever young.' He said: 'It *is* Tir na n-Og. They *have* the secret of perpetual youth. Did you ever see such clear eyes except in children? Did you ever see such ready smiles except in children, or such fun and pranks, such irresponsibility, and, at times, such naughtiness? They talk of a land that is far to the west, a land where they never grow old, where there is no consciousness of time. That land is here.'

In Galway, too, you find yourself talking to every one as if you had known them all your life. It is impossible to stand still in any one place in the town for two minutes without getting into conversation. When I was buying a few stamps in the post office a man, about to send a telegram, said to me: 'Did you hear about the bishop who came over from England to fish in Lough Corrib? He hadn't a bit of luck for days and days. Then, at last, he landed a trout. "D'you know," said he to the boatman, "that fish has cost me twenty pounds?" "Thin I hope to God ye don't catch another," said the boatman.' Probably an old story, probably told of many other lakes, but nowhere on shorter acquaintance than in Galway post office.

I was standing outside a hardware shop noting the different local patterns of spades, some with a single step, some 'eared' on both sides, some with straight sides, some tapering, when a woman said to me: 'Have you ever read De Quincey? Hasn't he the wonderful English? My husband is inside buying rat traps.'

Towards that same evening I asked a man if he could tell me the way to the college. 'Know the way to the college?' he said. 'If I was to take off me two boots and put them on the pavement before me, they'd find their own way there.' He lived less than half a mile further up the road, but he'd never been inside. He was 'no good at the books.' He would like to have travelled. Once he did have a mind to go to Ameriky, but when the time came he was 'wanting the courage.' So he had a drop of drink and when he woke up in the train 'twas in Dublin he was instead of Queenstown. 'Hadn't they a right to control me,' he asked, 'the same as an ox or a horse?' But they gave him a ticket back to Galway and he never left the town since. Then we got to talking about the weather. He said that 'Friday goes against all the rest of the week. If 'tis fine six days to Thursday it will be wet on Friday. If it is wet to Thursday it will be fine Friday.' But he didn't know what to think of the weather we'd been having. He'd never seen anything like it. 'The moment it's settled it changes.' I told him that it had been clear enough to see the Aran Isles that morning. 'If you can see the Arans,' he said, 'it's a sign of rain, and if you can't see them it's raining.'

Eventually we reached Maggie Ann Ashe's select bar where, within half an hour, I had accepted an invitation to go trawling with some of her fishermen clients. So, at five o'clock next morning, I found myself on the deck of their hooker, and we were sailing down the silver stream of the setting moon. And because there was a three hours' sail to the fishing grounds I lay down on the hatch, and, because it was January, the captain covered me with a sail. And I didn't wake till half-past seven when the dawn was breaking and the crew were preparing to shoot the trawl. And at eight o'clock they shot it, and then we had tea, and then we had the whole day before us to watch the gannets diving and the razor-bills skimming the waves and the gulls swooping and soaring. And at twelve o'clock we had more tea, and a potato or two, roasted on the stove in the cabin, and at half-past three they put the nose of the boat into the wind and hauled the trawl. And then the deck was alive with flapping fish, whiting, plaice, pollack, soles, and skate. And by the time they were packed, nine boxes in all, we were half-way up the bay, on the way home, and an hour later I was walking back to the hotel with a dozen plaice on a string.

'What will I give you for them?' asked Miss O'Carroll in the office.

'They're a present,' I said.

On my table, that night at dinner, there was a bottle of 1929 vintage Burgundy, and, on a card beside it: 'This is a present, too.'

CHAPTER FOUR

A LETTER REACHED ME. It was from a man in the town of Ennis. He claimed relationship with me on the ground that his aunt had been the second wife of my great-grandfather. He hoped that some day we would be friends as well as relations. And so we were.

It was in Ennis, on a fair day, that one of those peers with a double-barrelled name was seen crossing the square in a somewhat inebriated condition. 'Isn't that Lord "Clare and Galway"?' said one farmer to another. 'It is,' said the other, 'and both of them's drunk.'

I had passed through the town many years before, but I remembered little of it. My memories were chiefly of the country round about. In a village a few miles to the west my car had broken down. The bolt in the bottom of the sump had fallen out, and all the oil had gone. The only garage in the village was a small one, and the proprietor could find nothing to replace the missing screw. After two hours on his back on the dusty road he decided to plug the hole with wood which he lashed into place with wire and string. Then he filled up with oil.

'There you are now,' he said, 'that will carry you on a while.'

'How much do I owe you?' I asked.

'Oh, begod, you don't owe me anything.'

'And why not?'

'Oh, I couldn't charge you for that. Sure, I only made a temporary job of it.'

'But you've spent two hours on it.'

'Ah, it was a slack afternoon.'

'Well, how much do I owe you for the oil?'

'I couldn't rightly say the price of that.'

'I can tell you. It's so much a pint.'

'But it's cheaper by the gallon.'

Eventually I drove on, and in trying to pick up lost time I ran over a hen that was on the road and killed it. Leaving the corpse beside the car I went to the nearby cottage and knocked. A genial young man came to the door.

'I'm very sorry,' I said, 'but I've killed one of your hens.'

'I'm very much obliged to you,' he said.

'And what are you obliged for?'

' 'Twas very nice of you to come back and tell me.'

'Well, how much may I pay you?'

'Divil a penny, thin.'

'And what will I do with the hen?'

'Take her away with you, you're welcome.'

And so to Spanish Point on the coast. An aunt of mine owned a cottage there which she visited each summer with her family. That particular year I had taken a 'lodge' for my family. One half of the lodge was a thatched cottage, the other half was a castellated tower. We used to bathe from these houses, which were close to the shore, undressing and dressing indoors, and running to and from the sea in our bathing suits. One day my cousin Kathleen, having returned to her room, on the ground floor, had slipped off her wet garment and was getting busy with the towel when she noticed a shadow by the window. Looking out she saw one of the lads of the village. 'Get away out of that, Mickey,' she said. 'What are you doing there?' 'Arrah, Miss Kathleen,' said he, 'drop down that towel, sure you look lovely in your pelt.'

It was one of these men who found in his field of sprouting corn the hoof marks of a mare and foal, and that not on one morning only, but on several. It seemed to him a queer thing, for he knew well that the only mare and foal in the parish were stabled at night. So he and his son took watch, by turn, and two nights later what should the man hear but a whinny, and it coming up behind him from the

sea. It was full moon and, when he turned himself round, there on the rocks was a lovely mare with her foal, and they shaking the salt water off themselves. And, then, up they trotted to the oats, and made a trespass on them. The man was that surprised he kept hidden, and he never said a word that night. But the next day he told a wise man what he'd seen, and the wise man told him the mare was from the enchanted island of Hy Brazil. "Take with you a halter of sugawn," he said; "a straw rope it must be, and throw it over the mare's head and the enchantment will be broken, but mind you never let a common rope touch her neck or the spell will be on her again." So the man went away and made a sugawn halter, and that night he and his son kept watch, and, sure enough, they heard the whinny again, and this time there was a fine stallion along with the mare and foal, and all three of them trotted up to the oats. And the man was ready and he threw the straw halter over the neck of the stallion and caught him, but the mare and the foal flew back to the sea. Well, that stallion was the grandest animal and the finest worker in the countryside, and always a sugawn halter was used. But one day a new boy was working on the holding and he put a rope halter on the stallion. Up with his heels and a loud neigh he lets out of him and away into the sea with him and none of them was ever seen since.'

CHAPTER FIVE

FROM GALWAY I paid many visits to Connemara. To Ballynahown on the south coast, and to Maam Cross and Glendalough among the mountains, to Clifden and Ballyconneely in the west. On the day that I left for Ballynahown the bus was full, all except the two front seats, in one of which I sat. The other was taken soon after by an old man whose face was brown and wrinkled as well-worn shoe leather. Two bright blue eyes shone from deep in his head. He wore a bowler hat with a richly curved brim and a ribbon so frayed in front that it suggested a clerical rosette. Just as we were about to start a beggar woman got in. She came down the bus collecting pennies to right and left. As things happened I had nothing in my pocket less than a two-shilling piece. I couldn't be the only one to refuse, so, when it came to my turn, I gave her the silver. Immediately it was as if the heavens had opened, with the flood of blessings that were called down on my head. The whole bus was informed of what I had done. Wasn't I the real gentleman? Didn't she always say a real gentleman was worth a dozen others? Everybody stared at me. The conductor called to her to get out, but she took no notice of him. Saints and angels in scores were invoked on my behalf. The conductor called to her again. Still she paid no attention.

But at last we did get away. The old man on the opposite seat said nothing as we made our way out of the town, but I could see that he was watching me. Suddenly, in a loud voice, he called across the bus: 'Have you means?'

'I have not,' I said.

'Speak louder! I'm deaf.'

'I have not!' I shouted.

'How do you live?'

'Writing books.'

'You must have a great brain.'

Everybody in the bus was now listening. I tried to break off the conversation by looking out of the window, but there was no escape.

'You write books?' he called again.

'I do.'

'Would they bring you much?'

'Sometimes they would; sometimes they wouldn't.'

'How much would they bring you?'

Again I could feel the bus agog. 'It's hard to say,' I said.

'I can't hear you, I'm deaf!'

'It's hard to say,' I shouted.

'Would they bring you a pound in the week?'

'They might.'

'Would they bring you more?'

'They might, or they might not.'

Again I tried to look out of the window, but the inquisition went on.

'Have you been to Ameriky?'

'I have not.'

'Have you been to the Indies?'

'I have.'

'What took you there?'

'Writing a book.'

'You must have a power of learning.'

He paused a moment as if in wonder.

'Have you been to Australey?'

'I have.'

'How do they live?'

'Same as ourselves.'

'Have they sheep?'

'Thousands.'

'How many might one man have?'

'Fifteen thousand.'

'How can he count them?'

'Don't ask me.'

'What did you say?'

'I said, *Don't ask me.*'

'And what took you there?'

'Writing a book.'

'Another book! Glory be to God! Have you been to Borneo?'

'Never.'

'I'm told they murder you there and hang your scalp on their belt.'

'That's true,' I said, almost wishing he was there.

'We're better off in Ireland,' he said, getting up to go.

After the storm, a calm. The bus rolled on. Stones, stones, nothing but stones in the fields, rough stones, smooth stones, boulders with moss on them, pebbles glinting with quartz. In the road rocks rising like the slate-green backs of monsters from the sea. Wall after wall, so close that you wonder whether they are the boundaries of fields or the sides of ruined houses. Here and there stacks of turf where they could best meet drying winds. And, in the bog-lands, cattle on knolls or rocks to chew the cud.

At last it was time for me to get out. A boy was waiting to carry my bag. 'How do you shift the cattle from one field to another without any gates?' I asked.

'Wisha, push a bit of the wall down and build it up again. Isn't it as easy as to be lifting an old gate off its hinges?'

If a man were in search of a wilderness for a scapegoat he couldn't do better than survey the scenery a few miles to the west of Galway. How the cattle and sheep find a picking there it is hard to say. How the human creatures make a living is a greater wonder.

'But, sure, we're the richest people in the world,' said an old woman to me; 'the priest said that, because, he said, "we have the faith." 'Twas a great comfort to us when we heard it, indeed, you'd see the tears of joy in the people's eyes and they goin' down the road after mass.'

It was the time of the spring tides and the men were taking advantage of the low water. In their light home-spuns they were hardly distinguishable from the rocks, as they gathered weed along the shore. I spoke to several, but they had no English. I could only watch.

A young man sitting on the rump of a pony, behind two panniers, came down a lane at a gallop. The pony's bridle was no more than a rope tied over its head. The panniers hung from pegs in a wooden hames. A waterproof sheet over a thick layer of straw covered the animal's back. The pony stood while the dripping weed was loaded into the baskets, armful after armful alternately to each side. When the panniers were full more weed was piled on top between them, a rope was thrown across and fastened, and more weed piled still higher. Then another rope from the oppo-site side. As if the pony knew that its load was complete it started homeward across the loose stones before the last knot was tied.

Curraghs, like stranded whales, lay at the head of small beaches, beaches jewelled with shells. A net and a coil of rope, recently tanned, and now resting on a sheet of corrugated iron, drained their superfluous liquid back into the tan tub.

Along this coast it is considered most unlucky to save a man from drowning. 'The sea must have its due.' If you save a man, you or one of your family will most certainly be taken instead. The same belief is held in the Orkney and Shetland islands, and there are many people, on the east coast of Scotland, who will not even lift a dead body from the sea into a boat. 'It belongs to the sea.' Among some of the tribes of central and south-east Africa there is a similar reluctance to help a drowning man. To do so will bring misfortune on the rescuer. Closely connected with this idea was the custom among the vikings of Scandinavia, as it was also among many primitive people, to fasten one or more human beings to the rollers over which a ship, or war canoe, was launched. They were offerings to the sea. It was, no doubt, a survival of a similar belief that, till recently, caused two or more of the ship's apprentices to be ducked in the bow wave of the Peterhead whalers as they were launched from the shipyards at Aberdeen. Orkney boys fishing with the line throw back the first fish caught. It will bring luck, this offering of first fruits to the sea-god. And there are parallels to be found all over the world. In Morocco if the water in certain wells is scarce it will suddenly become plentiful if a person or animal falls into it. It may even be seen that the well wants 'a kill' by the way its water turns red. Only after some living creature has fallen into it does the water get back its natural colour. 'It craves a victim.' To-day, in the neighbourhood of Hay, on the Wye, children are warned not to play by the river lest the spirit pull them in. Not long ago, after a boy had been drowned near Ross, on the same river, somebody said that

it would be a lesson to his brothers not to go too near the
water, but an old man answered: 'Let 'em go, let 'em go.
The river has had its due.' In January 1904 a man was
drowned in the Derwent, in Derbyshire, because, it was believed, he had made light of the river. 'He said it were
nought but a brook. But Darrant got him. Nought but a
brook! He knows now.' In southern India there are rivers
whose spirits must be appeased by offerings of coin before
cattle can with safety be driven across. In Peru it was customary to throw maize into a stream as a propitiatory rite
before crossing. An even more extreme case of propitiation
of the elements comes from County Cork, where an old
man would always leave 'one little bit of a ridge of spuds
for the frost. Sure it must have something to eat,' he said.

While I was in Connemara a girl of about eighteen years
of age died of consumption. Her mother said to the doctor
who was attending her: 'Will you tell me, doctor, the
moment the soul is leaving the body?' He did so. Immediately the mother got up, closed the door of the room, and
plastered half a pound of butter along the crack between
the door and its frame. After a while she scraped off the
butter and put it in the fire. 'Now,' she said, 'we've caught
the evil, and we've burnt it; and it can do no more harm to
any one.'

On any of the small heather-bounded lakes that dot the
bogs swans may be seen, in pairs, in tens, in twenties. These
are the true wild swans, the whoopers and the Bewicks,
which, unlike the almost domestic mute swans of English
rivers and parks, have no black tubercles at the base of their
bills. Neither are the bills orange, as in the mute, but
lemon-gold, the gold of Lir's coronet; and their singing is
like to that of many women humming sadly, a sound weird
and mournful, interspersed with sighs and sobs, so that

those hearing it, after dark, will flee from the lake, fearing lest it be haunted.

Do you know the story of the children of Lir; how their stepmother, being jealous of the love that was shown to them by their father, Lir, turned them into swans, and how they remained thus for nine hundred years, until the coming of St. Patrick? Two things only she granted to them; that they should retain their human reason, without any grief for being in the shape of swans, and that they should still sing in their own Gaelic tongue. So, through all the centuries, they went from lake to lake, singing sweet plaintive music, the like of which was never heard in other lands. It excelled all the music of the world, and lulled to sleep every tired soul that heard it. And no man lifted a hand to hurt those swans, for the men of Ireland had made it a law that no man should kill a swan from that time forth, and no true man of Erin has ever done so to this day.

It was pouring rain, the day I returned to Galway, and I stood for half an hour, without shelter, waiting for the bus that was late. As if to make it later, we hadn't gone half a mile before a girl ran out of a cottage. 'Hold on a while, Taedy, till I do me hair,' she called to the driver. And so we tarried in our tracks.

As luck would have it, who should get into the bus at the next stop but my companion on the outward journey. And again he occupied the front seat on the right and I was in my same one on the left. For a while he said nothing, then suddenly he leaned towards me.

'Have you sold many books in Connemara?'

'Not many,' I said.

'Not many? That's bad!'

He was silent again for a few minutes, then, as if struck

with an idea, 'Tell me,' he said, 'are ye any good at writing love letters?'

'I've been lucky, an odd time,' I said.

'I got five pounds once for a love letter,' he said. 'I wrote it for a man west in Carraroe. He got the girl, and he got seven hundred pounds with her, and, faith then, he gave me five pounds for it. 'Tis a good line, mind you. You should try it.'

Before he could tender any more advice we were separated by two portly women in shawls, with baskets. Their conversation was about matrimony, and for the most part it was in Irish, which I did not understand, but every now and again they would break into English. One was apparently telling the other how her son had taken a liking for a girl in the town, 'but when I says to him: "How would she look under a cow?" sure, that finished him. He never threw a thought to her since.' Again there was some confidential chat, and then: 'But there's Mary Ryan is getting married, and him without as much as you'd jink on a tombstone, and that small you could blow him off the palm of your hand.'

'Ah, well, she's got one at last. Every morning for the past five years she's gone to mass, praying for a husband.'

And so we reached Galway. That evening the harper  was playing again. His wife was there too with her fiddle. If you would hear *The Old Rustic Bridge by the Mill* or *Teddy O'Neil*, played on the harp, across the wide square, in the soft evening light of the west, 'tis better for you to wear a wide-brimmed hat, for you may want to shade your eyes.

CHAPTER SIX

For contrast to the wilderness of stones and stone walls of southern Connemara one has only to travel inland a few miles from Galway to find a waste of moorland, with never a fence for mile on mile, and never a stone save the age-worn outcrops of silver granite. The bogs are every shade of brown and gold, the hills are every tint of purple, the only signs of green are a stray holly bush or the twigs of a stunted fir. Black bullocks munch the heather. Wild geese rise from the bog, their steel-grey backs the colour of the wind-swept lakes.

On all sides breath-taking glimpses of hill and pool. A robin sings to running water. Listen. Listen again. Tune your being to the song of streams. Close beside a fir-tree three sheep are grazing. Stand by the tree and think yourself into it. Touch it with the tips of your fingers. Lay the palms of your hands on its rough bark and feel the tremor of its fibres. Stretch up your spirit towards its topmost branches following each changing urge of growth. Sense its growth, for growth is immortality. We all are but cells, forming and re-forming in the elemental tissue, momentary manifestations, glimpses in the microscope of God. What does the chlorophyll cell in the blade of grass know of biology? Just as much, perhaps, as we do of eternity.

The robin is now in the brushwood. The wind has dropped. There isn't a breath to stir the rushes, the cloud shadows stand as they fell on the hills. The road curves like the hollow of a thigh, the mountains rise like the swelling of a breast, the pools are clear as kittens' eyes.

I spoke of geese. Geese, said to be the most faithful to their mates of all living creatures. Among many anecdotes the following, told by W. H. Hudson in his *Birds and Man*, is typical. It was narrated to him by his brother, a sheep farmer in South America. 'Immense numbers of upland geese in great flocks used to spend the cold months on the plains where he had his lonely hut; and one morning in August in the early spring of that southern country, some days after all the flocks had taken their departure to the south, he was out riding, and saw at a distance before him on the plain a pair of geese. They were male and female— a white and a brown bird. Their movements attracted his attention and he rode to them. The female was walking steadily on in a southerly direction, while the male, greatly excited, and calling loudly from time to time, walked at a distance ahead, and constantly turned back to see and call to his mate, and at intervals of a few minutes he would rise up and fly, screaming, to a distance of some hundreds of yards; then finding that he had not been followed, he would alight at a distance of forty or fifty yards in advance of the other bird, and begin walking on as before. The female had one wing broken, and, unable to fly, had set out on her long journey to the Magellanic Islands on her feet; and her mate, though called too by that mysterious impera- tive voice in his breast, yet would not forsake her; but fly- ing a little distance to show her the way, and returning again and again, and calling to her with his wildest and most piercing cries, urged her still to spread her wings and fly with him to their distant home. And in that sad, anxious way they would journey on to the inevitable end, when a pair or family of carrion eagles would spy them from a great distance—the two travellers left far behind by their fellows, one flying, the other walking; and the first would be left to continue the journey alone.'

But in fairness to other species of birds I must not omit a story of a peregrine falcon's affection for its mate told by P. H. Bahr in *British Birds* (May 1908). The female had been wounded and had fallen to the ground with both legs broken. It was in January, during a hard frost, and her wings, stretched out, had become frozen to the ground. Around her lay the remains of wild duck, partridges, and pheasants, while above her hovered her mate. From the state of her injuries it was reckoned that she must have been in that position for over a fortnight, yet, thanks to the care of her mate, she was in almost perfect condition when found.

Of the virtues of geese, the late J. G. Millais wrote that of all birds, they are the most intelligent. 'Conspicuous, too, are they for bravery and domestic affection. In the particular art of defending themselves against the wiles of the fowler, whether afloat, or ashore, they have absolutely no equal.' As an instance of the latter he tells how, on one occasion, when he found himself within about a hundred and fifty yards of a flock of some six hundred birds, a mixture of greylags, pinkfoots, and bean geese, he noticed five or six birds who 'kept on the alert the whole time, walking about quickly and suspiciously on all four sides of the main body and never attempting to feed.' He goes on to say that after watching them for about ten minutes he saw, distinctly, 'a goose which had been busily eating go up to one of the sentinels and touch him on the back with his bill. Immediately the sentry lowered his head and commenced to pick at the grass, while the goose who had just been feeding raised his neck and began to keep watch. It was their mode of changing sentry.' After this he 'kept particular watch on the sentries, and twice again saw other geese come up, peck them in a friendly sort of way, as much as to say "I'll do my turn now," and thus relieve the look-out of his duty.' It is told, too, that if a human being, in order to entice them, puts down food in one of their usual feeding places the geese will leave that place instead of staying. But, then, the expression 'a wild-goose chase' has become a proverb. So has the watchfulness of geese, ever since the days of Rome, 390 B.C. To-day any farmer will tell you that a goose is the best 'watch-dog.' In an issue of *The Times* during 1940 we read that before ever the sirens had sounded and before the human ear could catch the drone of an aeroplane there occurred 'an outburst of angry cackling from these historic sentinels.'

Swans rise heavily and with effort, ducks rise with a flurry, but geese lift themselves majestically into the air. It may be hard to guess how certain collective terms have arisen for other birds and animals, but there can be little doubt about 'a gagelyng of geese.' 'Gaggle-gaggle, gaggle-gaggle' is the sound one hears, high overhead, almost a flock chuckle as they pass far out of range. In this connection I like, too, the terms 'a paddling of ducks,' in old English 'a padelynge of dookysse,' 'a murmuration of starlings,' 'a congregation of plovers.'

Dotted about the bogs are stacks of brown turf. Here and there the dark walls of peat faces rise from pools of black oily water. In the peat face may be seen the stems and branches of trees long buried. *Vir* or bogwood, they call it. 'The best kindling in the world.' Almost straight from the bog it will light. A twig when dried will burn as a candle. 'It's the oil that's in it from the turf.'

Turf is cut with a slane, a narrow spade with an ear at right angles to the blade so that two sides of the sod are cut at the same time from the stepped face of the bog. Each newly cut sod is like a large brick, dark and oily. A good slanesman will cut close on three thousand of them in one day, that is to say, about four tons of turf. But this turf is 'raw.' It must be spread to dry as hay is spread, cocked as hay is cocked, and stacked into clamps as hay is built into ricks. Finally, it must be thatched with straw even as hay-ricks are thatched against the weather. A ton of raw turf yields but three hundredweight of fuel. Each year the cutting begins when the winds of March have dried the bogs. If that crop can be saved in time, a second harvest is cut in July.

Bogs hold more than turf and bogwood. It is a commonplace that bronze implements of all kinds have been found in them. Scarcely a museum that has not a specimen of one kind or another, preserved by the bacteria-free soil, of wooden bowls and platters, goblets, spades, spoons, canoes, and paddles; not to mention items of ancient dress such as cloaks and tunics of wool, capes of skin, or shoes of leather. One of the largest dug-out canoes ever found in western Europe, fifty-two feet in length, was taken from a bog in County Galway.

But one of the most surprising, though by no means uncommon, finds is bog butter. This is not, as one might suspect by the name, some strange fungus akin to the yellow jelly-like growth found on trees, and known as witch's butter, but the genuine churn-made product of the milk of cows, sometimes still edible. Knowing the preservative power of bogs its owners had buried it, to await such time as they were going to market, four, five, or six months ahead. Meanwhile, death or accident intervened, and so the wooden firkin, or the skin or cloth container, with its contents, lay undisturbed, fifty, a hundred, maybe two hundred, years.

CHAPTER SEVEN

I HAD BEEN 'travelling light,' lighter than I thought, for one evening, after a leap across a stream, I found myself through both knees of my trousers. There was nothing to do but cut off the extremities of the garment and travel in shorts.

'I have a bit of tweed might suit you,' said my hostess at the hotel, a day or two later. 'I've had it this long while. If it's any good to you, you're welcome.'

'But where could I get it made up?'

'We'll send over for Taedy. Paddy!' she called, to a boy who was sweeping out the yard. 'Paddy, get on to your bike and go over tell Taedy there's a gentleman wants a suit.'

Paddy set out as he was told.

'Has he far to go?' I asked.

' 'Tis no more than eight miles across the mountains.'

Taedy arrived that afternoon. He was a fresh-faced, fair-haired young man. When he saw me his blue eyes sparkled. But he said nothing. He came across the room and walked round me twice. He ran his fingers across my shoulders, and pulled at the tail of my coat. Still he said nothing; but he clapped his hands. Then he took an old envelope from his pocket and wrote on the back of it: 'Your backbone will never cut your shirt.' Then he clapped his hands again.

(47)

Writing was his only means of communication. He was a deaf mute.

He disentangled a measuring tape from a collection of string that was in his pocket and began to take measurements. Suddenly, in a quite irrelevant way, he wrote: 'The crows will soon be building.' While I read that he took another measurement. Then he continued: 'They start on the 1st March. If that's a Sunday they wait till the 2nd.' While he was on his knees dealing with my trousers he wrote: 'If you get the rheumatics boil a heron and rub in the oil.'

As he was leaving I inquired what the cost of the suit would be.

'Twenty-four and six for the making. Can you manage it?'

I nodded.

He clapped his hands, patted me on the shoulder, and wrote 'You're in the middle of plenty.' Then he added: 'Fitting on Thursday?' Again I agreed. He shook my hand, went outside, got on to his bicycle, and was away with the tweed into a southerly gale of wind and rain, in the gathering darkness.

On the Thursday I had a chance of reaching his house before he had left it to visit me. It was a blustering day, with glimpses of turquoise blue through towering clouds. After each spatter of rain diamonds glistened on the hedge side. We drove by roads beside lake margins, through wastes of sheep-nibbled heather. Only on the islets which stud the lakes was there heavy vegetation. There, ungrazed, the long grasses waved and the thickly woven trees stood snug, trimmed only by the winds.

Taedy's cottage was bare of all furniture except a table and a few low chairs. On the table was a sewing-machine.

In the open hearth a tailor's iron was heating in the turf fire. A small oil lamp hung on the wall. A religious picture was the only decoration.

While fitting he interrupted his work constantly to write down fragments of thought on scraps of paper. ' 'Tis a short visit we pay to this world.' 'Fasting spit will cure anything.' 'If the fairies get you, turn your coat inside out.' 'My grandfather never had an overcoat. He died at a hundred and two.' 'People to-day wear as many coats on them as an onion.'

Eventually the fitting was over. The suit would be ready next week. He'd bring it over. He liked the fresh air in his face and the wind to be combing his hair. As he wrote this he patted his cheeks to show how the wind reddened them. As I was leaving he handed me a tattered child's exercise book, and wrote: 'Will you put your name in the book so I'll make a record of it for ever.'

CHAPTER EIGHT

ANOTHER LETTER of invitation came from Patrick Flannery of Ballinrobe. Though we had never met we had corresponded. Indeed, it was he who had told me the story which I wrote in *Sweet Thames* of the little fairy woman that he had seen coming to the edge of the lake for water. Now he wrote asking when I was coming to Ballinrobe, and saying that he had a boat on Lough Mask which was mine for as long as I wanted it.

So, a few weeks later, I stepped out of the bus at Ballinrobe, and he was there to meet me; warm and genial, a man who, during a long life, had never lost an opportunity to wonder.

He had booked a room for me at Moran's Hotel, and Mrs. Moran was at the door to greet me. 'Come in, now,' she said. 'You must be tired? Of course you are. Come in

(50)

now, and sit down. Relax. Put your feet up. Relax, that's what I always say. You'd like a little something? You would to be sure. A large one? Yes, of course!'

'How much is that?' I asked, a moment later.

'Ah, nothing at all. Sure that's on the house, just to welcome you.'

I stayed in that hotel for six weeks and there was scarcely a day when I wasn't given 'a little something' for one reason or another. 'Sure, we can't be making a profit out of you all the time.'

Ballinrobe, in Irish Baile-an-Rodba, meaning 'The Town on the (river) Robe,' is in the County Mayo, in Irish Maigh-Eo, meaning 'The Plain of the Yews.' It is not a large town, neither is it pretentious. It is as unpretentious as an open hearth, but as warm and friendly. Everybody is ready for a talk at any hour, in any place, and after five minutes it is: 'If there's anything I can do for you let me know.'

Pat Flannery and I were soon friends. The length of our steps and the speed of our movements matched each other like the four legs on a dog. We walked towards the sun in the morning, and we came back towards the sun in the evening. We walked with the south wind in our faces at noon, and we looked up at the pole-star on our way home.

There was the road to Lough Mask. Less than a mile from the town is Tober-Mhuire, the Well of Mary, under its thorn trees, and surrounded by its ivy-covered wall. Here pilgrims come to make their rounds and ask a favour of the Blessed Virgin.

Half a mile further on the road stands a cairn, the memorial to a chief who died and was buried a thousand years before the time of Christ. Two hundred paces in circumference, stone upon stone piled high, each one a warrior's

lament. Now the stones shine with golden and silver
lichens, and rough places are made smooth with ferns and
saxifrages and stonecrops. 'All the grand monuments in the
world tumble away, but a heap of stones lasts for ever,' said
Flannery.

Over the brow of the next hill there is Michael O'Con-
nor's sand pit. 'Two sackfuls of bones they dug out of that.
Some were buried stretched, and some were buried with
their knees up agin their chests, and there's more of them
were burnt and buried inside of urns,' we were told. Altogether ten burials had been found, of which seven had been
in single cist-graves, two in double-compartmented cists,
and one unprotected, but with a pillar stone three feet six
inches high marking the grave. Four of the cists had held
'urns,' not cinerary urns but food vessels, of which three
had rested inverted over the cremated bones. In one case
among the bones there was a small flint knife, highly
worked on one side, but with the natural cleavage face on
the other side untouched.

The one cist that remained when I was there had been built of half a dozen flat stones, four of them forming the sides, and the others the top and bottom of the cavity. Of this I was able to make a drawing before it also gave way to the needs of a building contractor. It is interesting to note that the manufacture of food vessels such as those found in these graves was one of the duties of the women of the

community, a fact gleaned from the finger-prints of the maker, often to be seen in the clay. When the potter's wheel came into use at a later date the work devolved upon the men. The date of these particular interments was probably between 1600 B.C. and 1400 B.C., but the three different kinds of burial, bodies straight, bodies flexed, others cremated, may indicate that the site had been used as a cemetery, at intervals, over a considerable period of time.

Beyond the sand pit there's a corner where 'many a man gets a weakness. 'Tis there they'd put down the coffin for a rest when they'd be carrying it to the church-yard.'

On this road, too, there is a cave, 'The Bed of Dermat and Grania,' one of the many resting places of those lovers, Dermat a warrior of untarnished honour and Grania the daughter of a king, who fled from the wrath of Finn, the son of Cumal, whose desire was upon Grania. From Tara to Athlone they went and thence to Galway. From Galway to the 'Wood of the Two Sallows,' now known as Limerick, and from Limerick to the river Laune that flows from Kil-larney to the sea. From there to the wild Dingle peninsula and then, at last, after many wanderings, to Sligo, where for a time they found peace. Great was his strength, great was his courage, great was his tenderness. Only in the latter end, through treachery, was he slain, and then by a wild boar, that boar whose head many branches of the Campbell Clan now carry as their crest, they being descended from 'Dermat O'Dyna, of the Bright Face, a valiant champion, of surpassing beauty, the favourite of maidens.'

In a field to the west of the cave there is a thorn-tree with a slab of stone under it, and under that slab there is a great treasure buried. But if any one touches the stone, to get at the treasure, three men will die in the parish. So the stone and the treasure lie undisturbed.

And again to the west by a side-road, it would be five miles from Ballinrobe, there is Lough Mask Castle, built in the thirteenth century. Much of it, however, was rebuilt three hundred years later, as the dates on two fireplaces still show. Among other owners the castle at one time be-longed to the Bourkes, descendants of the Norman De Burgos. After the battle of Aughrim in 1691 when, for the time being, the Irish were defeated, the Bourke of that day found himself a prisoner in the Tower of London. 'But he was a very nice sort of a fellow and he got to be friendly with the guards in the Tower, and from one day to another they'd be bringing him the news. And one day they told him of a great fighter who was challenging the world, to fight him with a sword. And no one would take him on for he'd killed every man he'd ever met. "Faith, I'll take him on," said Bourke. "You will?" said the guard. "I will," said Bourke. So the news came to the king that there was a man willing to fight and the king came down to see Bourke in the Tower. "How long would it take you," said the king, "to get strong, for the prison food is none too good?" " 'Twould take a month with the best of food," said Bourke. So the king gave orders that he was to have all the food he wanted and all the exercise he wanted. "The best of everything," said the king. And at the end of the month the king came down to the Tower to see Bourke again. "Are you ready?" said he. "I am," said Bourke. "Come down to the armoury now and choose a sword," he said. So down the two of them went and one sword after another was shown to Bourke, and Bourke made slashes in the air with them all, and every one of them snapt off at the hilt. "I must have my own sword," said Bourke. "Where is it?" said the king. "Back at Lough Mask Castle," said Bourke. " 'Tis in the chest in the hall, on the left as you go in at the front door," he said. So the king sent off two special couriers to fetch the sword. "Faith, 'tis driving again in my carriage and pair I'll be," said Mrs. Bourke, when she seen the two men, "for," said she, "there isn't a man alive could stand up to Bourke." Well 'twas a great fight and the king and all the nobles and the ladies and the court were there to watch, and the two of them slashed away at each other all day, without ever a

sign of the one or the other weakening, until the evening.
All of a sudden a fellow in the crowd called out to Bourke.
"Remember Aughrim," he called. With that, the fire
blazed up in Bourke's eyes and with one slash of his sword
he took the head clean off the other fellow. Well, you may
say they were all delighted. Then the king comes down to
Bourke.

'"Bourke," said he, "you're free. Go home," said he,
"and get the fastest horse you can," said he, "and ride from
dawn till dusk, and all the land that you encircle is yours."
And that's how the Bourkes came to own all their land.
But they've lost the most of it since.'

How true the details of this story may be is difficult to
say. Something very similar is told of John de Courcy, Earl
of Ulster, in the time of King John. But in his case there
was no fight. One stern look from de Courcy was enough
for his adversary who, without further ado, put spurs to his
horse, broke through the barrier, and was never heard of
again. Then was granted to the de Courcys that privilege,
which they still retain, of remaining 'covered' in the royal
presence.

But before leaving Lough Mask Castle there is other history to be told, for it was in the house adjoining the castle
that there lived Captain Boycott, a man whose name has
become noun and verb in the English language. That was
in the year 1880, a tragic time in Ireland's history, a time of
starvation, and eviction of people unable to pay their rent
through repeated failure of the potato crop. In 1878 there
had been seventeen hundred and forty-nine of these evic-
tions, and in 1879 the number had risen to two thousand
six hundred and sixty-seven. Boycott was agent to Lord
Erne. In the midst of all the distress he refused to accept the
rents that the tenants were able to offer, demanding the

full amounts due, and, in default thereof, issuing processes of ejectment. What could the people do but retaliate? No labourer would work for him. No tradesman would supply goods. The smith would not shoe his horses, the post-boy would not deliver letters. Pictures in the *Graphic* of 20th November 1880 show the captain driving his own reaping machine while four female relatives gather the mown corn into sheaves. Armed police stand by. Other pictures of the same time show the arrival of relief labourers, escorted by hussars, 'Morning inspection of the Royal Dragoons at Ballinrobe,' 'Social relaxation of the Light Horsemen,' sad groups of families looking back at their cottages guarded by police. Finally, we see Captain Boycott and his family, complete with their parrot in its cage, leaving Lough Mask House in a Red Cross wagon, accompanied by a troop of cavalry. If these pictures are as true as the portrait of Valkenburg's Hotel in the town, still going strong, we need no further evidence to visualize the whole story.

From one extreme to another. While studying these pictures I came across the following reference to military life at the Curragh Camp. 'Most of the huts of the married officers are marvellously and dexterously fitted up, more especially the drawing-rooms. The greatest possible taste and ingenuity are displayed in their interior arrangements. Scarcely a scrap of wall-paper is left uncovered or un-adorned. China plates with velvet backgrounds of quaint device, carved brackets, mirrors, reflecting glasses, book-cases with gold-embossed doors. Birds' nests are grouped artistically along the walls, whilst Japanese fans and um-brellas depend grotesquely from the corners of the ceilings. . . . One room, which struck us with unusual admiration, was entirely decorated, covered, to speak accurately, with every shade of blue and green, the velvet background of each mirror and each ornament being also embellished with peacocks' feathers arranged according to the fancy of its mistress.' And so on for several paragraphs.

But I think it is time for a new chapter.

CHAPTER NINE

THERE ARE MANY ISLANDS in Lough Mask, and few of them are without history. Inishowen takes its name from Eoghan, who reigned over Connaught during the early part of the sixth century. In a battle against the men of the north, A.D. 537, he was mortally wounded, though we are told by his son, who afterwards became St. Ceallach, that he survived the battle for three days. Before dying, he called his warriors to him. 'Bury me,' he said, 'standing in my grave, with my face to the north, and with my spear and my shield in my hands, for as long as I stand facing them, they cannot gain the mastery.' And so it was for many days. But when the men of the north heard what had been done, they came by night, stealthily, and stole away the body, carrying it with them into the plains of Sligo. And there they buried the dead king in the low ground, with his face downward, ignobly. Thus was the spell broken.

But Dun Eoghan still stands upon Inish Eoghan. It is there for all to see, with its ring of standing stones among the trees that crest the hill.

On Inishmaine, Middle Island, there are the remains of an early monastery and of an ancient castle. There is also a curious structure whose purpose had hitherto been in some doubt. It consists of an almost solid rectangular block of

unmortared masonry some fifteen feet long and wide and
about twelve in height, in which are two crypts, each about
seven feet long, three feet wide, and five feet high at the
apex of their high-pitched roofs. The floors of these crypts
are of flat stones stretching from side to side, with sufficient
space under them and between them for air to pass. Sir
William Wilde, whose *Lough Corrib* is still the standard
work on the archaeology of this district, was of opinion that
the building 'may have been a prison, or penitentiary, in

which some of the refractory brethren of the neighbouring
abbey were confined.' He could imagine unfortunate
brothers stretched for long hours on the cold slabs of stone,
expiating their sins, whereas, in all probability, it was on
straw or rushes over roasting hot stones that they lay, in the
hope of exorcising their rheumatics or other pains. He
stated that there was neither history nor legend attached to
the place. It only needed an ounce of tobacco, on my part,
to discover that there is still a very definite legend that the
place was once a sweat-house, a primitive form of the more
elegant Turkish baths of to-day. With that idea in my mind
I obtained a sample of the soil from beneath the floor stones
and had it analysed. 'Charred fragments of rushes and straw
impregnated with crystals of sodium chloride, which latter
could only be from sea water or human sweat,' was the gist

of the report. As the sea is many miles away and the lake is above sea-level it is not unreasonable to assume that the crystals are from sweat. The charred fragments would be from the layers of rushes and straw laid on the hot stones before the patient entered.

Sweat-houses were not uncommon in Ireland in early times and had much in common with those in use in many other countries. In Russia 'the bathing establishment usually consisted of a small wooden structure in which was built a vaulted oven. On the top of this oven were a number of paving stones, which became red hot when the oven was heated. Alongside the oven was a boiler containing hot water. All around the room, rising in tiers, were benches upon which the bathers sat or reclined. . . . Every few minutes water from the boiler was thrown over the red-hot stones, causing dense vapour to arise, and increasing the temperature to as much as 130 degrees.' After some minutes of profuse perspiration an attendant washed the bather's body, following this with massage and a scourging with leafy birch twigs. In Finland something of the same kind occurred. Among the North American Indians the patient sat in a kind of basket over red-hot stones on which water was thrown, thereby becoming enveloped in steam. The Turks elaborated the Russian and Finnish technique into a system of kneading and pummelling known as shampooing. In nearly all cases, after achieving a profusion of sweat it was customary for the patient to take a plunge either into a stream or a lake or, as in Finland and Russia, a roll in the snow. If Lough Mask seems a long run from the sweat-house at Inishmaine it is only because in recent years, by artificial means, the level of the lake has been lowered.

Mr. James Buckley, M.R.I.A., writing on this subject of baths a few years ago, says: 'When the Roman legions were

withdrawn from Britain towards the middle of the fifth
century the bath fell into disuse in that country, and so for
fourteen centuries the bath ceased to exist in England, its
use was entirely unknown. Yet it is an interesting and
singular fact that during this period a rude adaptation of
the principles of the bath existed in Ireland, and was highly
prized by the people. It is impossible to determine how a
knowledge of the principle of the hot-air or oriental bath
reached Ireland. It is certain, however, that a rude form of
bath on that principle has been in existence from very remote ages. If, as supposed, the Phoenicians ever visited
Ireland, they may have brought a knowledge of the bath
with them from the East; or during the Roman occupation
of Britain, their use of the bath may have become known
to the Irish.'

In the year 1850 Mr. David Urquhart, M.P., published,
in London, a work in two volumes, *The Pillars of Hercules,*
which contained chapters descriptive of the baths used by
the Turks and Moors. Inspired by what he had read in that
work Dr. Richard Barter, of St. Ann's Hill, County Cork,
built there the first Turkish bath to be erected in modern
Europe. Its reputation spread to such an extent that similar
institutions soon sprang up in England, America, France,
and Germany. Hence the title 'Römische-Irische Bäder'
which may be seen in many towns in Germany to-day.

Earl's Island is so called since the son of the Earl of
Ulster was murdered there in 1338. 'Dropped into the lake,
he was, in a sack.' Roderick O'Flaherty, the seventeenth-
century chronicler, records that it was members of the
Anglo-Norman family of de Stauntons, said to have come
originally from Warwickshire, who committed the deed.
'Within that arm of Lough Measg is the Earl's Island where
Edmond Burke, second son of Richard, the Red Earl of

Ulster, A.D. 1338 was put to death. . . . This Edward was joyned in commission with Malachias, Archbishoppe of Tuam, for the government of Connaught, until he was seized by Sir William Bourke's sons on Low Sunday, the 19th of April, in the Friars house of Ballinrobe. . . . He was carried that night to Lough Measg Castle, the next night to Ballyndeonagh Castle, and the third night to that island in Lough Measg: whither the Archbishoppe of Tuam came to bring him and his kinsmen to a reconciliation; and as they were on point of agreement, the villains who had the custody of him, a certain family of the Stauntons, despairing their own safety if he were set at liberty, miserably turned him into a bag and cast him out of the island into the lake with stones tied to the bag: for which fact they [that family] were called Clan Ulcin [meaning 'the children of evil'] ever since. Hence followed great combustions and wars in Connaught after.'

Castle Hag, 'the earliest castle in Ireland' according to Sir William Wilde, stands on another island. It takes its name from the numbers of shags, or cormorants, which at one time nested there. The castle, noted in history before the Anglo-Norman conquest, was demolished by one Felim O'Conor in A.D. 1233, but about a century later it was rebuilt by the de Burghs. In 1586 Sir Richard Bingham, of unblessed memory in Ireland, laid siege to it and destroyed it.

'I think we'll have a bit of a smoke,' said Flannery, one day after we had landed on this island. Michael Quinn, who owns a cottage beside the lake, had come with us to troll a line for trout. But he had caught nothing. Now, as we sat amid the ruins, a robin and a butterfly were the only signs of animal life besides ourselves. But the uncropped grass grew rich and high, the gorse shone gold, and ever in our

ears was the fugue-like music of the lake. Flannery and
Quinn filled their pipes and lit them.

'Michael,' said Flannery.

'Yes, Pat.'

'Michael, did I ever tell you what happened to Shawn
Riordan, and he on his way home one night?'

'You did not, Pat.'

'Then I'll tell you now.'

The two of them puffed away at their pipes. Gulls were
in the air. A pair of mallard flew high overhead, five tufted
duck, nearer to the water, passed down the lake. They do
not nest as early as the mallard. In contrast to the quick
flapping of the ducks, how serene the slow sailing of the
gulls.

'Well,' said Flannery, 'Shawn was going home late one
night after a wake, and on his way he had to pass a big high
wall, as high as yourself it was. And as he was passing, what
did he hear from inside the wall but a lot of shouting. So he
puts his foot in a hole in the wall and he climbs up and he
looks over, and what did he see but two teams of little men
and they playing hurley. And there he stood for a long
while with his foot in the hole in the wall, watching them.
All of a sudden one of the little fellows climbs up the other
side of the wall, and stretching out two of his fingers, he
points them at Shawn's eyes. "Go home," he said, "or I'll
blind you." Those were his very words. "Go home, or I'll
blind you." You may bet Shawn ran away home pretty
quick. Sure I knew him well, and he often told it to me.'

'Well,' said Michael, 'I can tell you what was told to me
by a parish priest, and it happened to a man he knew, so it
must be true. It was not far from Doonlaun near Shrule,
and it was to a man of the name of Tom Monahan that it
happened. Tom was one of the finest hurlers in the district,

and one bright moonlight night he was on his way home, and he had to pass by a field that sloped down from a wood, in the face of the moon. What was his surprise to see two teams of men playing hurley. Well, he watched, and he watched, and after a while it came to him that they were the good people. And they were playing wonderful, and he stood for a long while admiring their play, until in the latter end, with the dint of delight that he had in a great stroke, he let out a shout from him. Then they all knew he was there, and him a mortal.

' "Would you like to join in?" asked one of them, as nice as you please.

' "I would, indeed," said Tom, "but is there a place for me?"

' "There is surely," said they, "for there's a gap in one side."

' "Have you a hurley?" asked Tom.

' "Here's the best," said they, handing one to him. A lovely stick it was.

'So Tom played, and he played as never before, and his side won the match.

' "I'll tell you who we are now," said the good people, for they were very friendly with Tom. "We are from the churchyard beyond. But," they added, "we are in a great fix, for we have to play our old rivals from Knockma on this night week, and they've got a mortal, the red-headed Paddy, Paddy Ruadh, to play for them, and he is the best hurler in Mayo. Could you help us?" said they.

' "I could," said Tom, "but could I have the same hurley?"

' "You can," said they.

'So a week from that night Tom crept out, telling no one where he was going, and he reached the same field, and there were the two teams, and his hurley was waiting for him. And they played and they played, and in the finish Tom's team won, and there was great joy in his team.

'"What would you like now, and we'll give it to you?" they said. "Anything you'd like at all?"

'"I'd like that hurley," said Tom. "'Tis the finest hurley I ever played with," he said, "for I never missed a ball, high or low, with it."

'"That's true enough," they said. "You never missed a ball, high or low, but you've asked the one thing we can't do. 'Tis fairy property and we couldn't give it away."

'Tom was kind of hurt at this and he was an obstinate sort of a fellow.

'"I must have it," he says.

'"You can't," they said.

'"I must," said Tom.

'With that there was a great altercation, and, in the end, Tom walked off, taking the hurley with him.

'Well, Tom was hardly home before he began to sicken. His mother could do nothing for him, and the doctor could do nothing for him.

'"Is there anything at all that you'd wish?" said his mother to him one day.

'"There's a hurley up in the rafters," said he. "Will you bring it down and put it on the end of the bed so I can see it?" he said.

'And all the time he grew worse and worse. And when they seen that he was going to die, "Have you any last wish at all?" they said.

'"Promise me one thing," he said.

'"We will," they said.

'"Promise me," he said, "to put that hurley in the coffin alongside of me."

'Sure enough they did it. So maybe he's still winning matches for Doonlaun.'

The two men puffed at their pipes.

'Some say they only appear to you if the priest forgot a word or two of the service when he was christening you,' said Flannery.

'I think it's according to the time of day that you were born,' said Quinn. 'There was a boy at school with me beyond in the village. He was born on Good Friday and baptized on Easter Sunday, and he was the seventh son. One day at school he saw a worm and he drew a circle around it on the ground with his finger, and he made the sign of the Cross over it, and the worm died on the spot. When the boy's father heard about it, he beat hell out of him for it, and the boy never did the like again. But you should hear Patsy Whelan,' he added.

'We'll go over to-morrow,' said Flannery to me.

CHAPTER TEN

'GOD SAVE ALL HERE,' said Pat Flannery. 'God save all here,' said I, as the two of us bent our heads and went in at the door of Patsy Whelan's cottage about eight o'clock on the following evening.

'And ye, too,' answered Patsy. He was a little old man of close on eighty years of age. His face was a mass of brown wrinkles, but the bald top to his head was shining white. A wisp of grey hair hung over each ear and a fringe of it over the back of his collar, otherwise his head was bare. He

had the fire tongs in his hand when we arrived, and he was
putting small bits of red turf on the lid of a pot that hung
over the smouldering side of a double hearth. His daughter
had gone out and left him to cook 'the cake.' A brighter
fire was burning alongside, under another pot, a larger one,
that held a mash for the pigs. We sat listening to the
crickets chittering in the hearth. Sometimes when a flame
spurted up we could see these grasshopper-like creatures
scuttling among the ashes.

'They're after taking a pair of them to Bridie Sweeney's
new house over at Kilmaine,' said Patsy. 'They bring luck.'

'Did you know,' I said, 'that they can make all that noise
by merely scraping one limb against another?'

'I did not,' he said.

He pulled two pieces of a clay pipe from his pocket, the
bowl and the stem that had been broken from it. 'Did you
know,' he said, 'that you can mend a broken pipe with
blood?'

'I did not,' I said.

'Nor did I till I saw Teigue O'Reilly do it last week.'

He got up and fumbled about the house for a pin. He
inquired if either of us had one, without success. 'May we
never want for more,' he said, going out of the door.

A moment later he came back with a bramble. With this
he scratched the back of his hand and with the blood that
flowed he joined the broken ends of the pipe, holding them
together in the warmth of the fire. 'That'll be better than
a new pipe to-morrow,' he said, laying it carefully among
the plates on the dresser. Then he came back and sat down
by the fire.

'Draw up a bit closer,' he said, 'the nights do be peevish.'

We sat in to the fire and we watched the silent flames.
Turf is such a gentle burner. When a great glowing cavity

formed in the heart of the fire, Patsy would take the tongs
and push a fresh sod in to fill the space.

Mary, the daughter, came in. She lifted the pot from its
hook, shook the ash off the lid into the hearth, and took the
flat soda-bread loaf from inside. Bastaple bread they call it.

'Danny will be late,' said Patsy.

'He will,' said Mary. 'I'm going over to Dempsey's a
while.' She pulled a shawl over her head and went out.

'Going over to Dempsey's! And Danny dancing beyond
at Knockma,' said Patsy thoughtfully. ' 'Twas working for
Con Dempsey's uncle over at Knockma that the queerest
thing ever happened to any man happened to me. After
I'd been dancing, too. D'you know that big barn, below in
the lane, to the east of the fork roads, this side of the castle?'

'I do,' said Flannery.

'Well, 'twas there we were threshing, threshing with the
flail in them days, good flails with a handle of ash and a
beater of holly. And we'd been at it all day, and we'd left
everything as it stood, overnight, and there was a dance this
side of Ardrumkilla and we all went to it. And next morning I was coming home, and I was travelling the last part
of the road, and I was alone, and 'twas four o'clock in the
morning, and I was passing the lane to the barn, and I was
thinking will I go home to bed. But, if I do, I said, I'll surely
sleep through the day and I'll lose me job. So I went down
the lane to the barn, thinking to myself that, maybe, I'd
have a bit of a snooze in the straw, or, maybe, do a little bit
of extra work in the early morn. But, when I gets to the
barn, what do I hear but music, dance music, the music of
the pipes and the fiddle coming out of the barn. And I was
wild, for what would they be doing in there, trampling the
corn and destroying it, when 'twas all spread for threshing.
So I crept up and I peeped in through a chink in the

boards. Faith, the light nearly went out of me eyes. There was fairies galore. And they were dancing. And the floor was swept clean, and it was a good floor, too, for it belonged to the manor house. And the fairies were dancing there like mad. Well, I watched and I watched, when, all of a sudden, I let out a sneeze. I suppose 'twas a speck of the dust got into me nose. The very next thing, didn't one of them throw a handful of chaff in me face, and when I got the use of me eyes there wasn't sight nor sound of them, and the floor, the same as ever we'd left it, with the sheaves laid out for the morning's threshing.'

'And there's some,' I said, 'that don't believe in fairies!'

'There was a man I knew,' said Patsy, 'who said he didn't believe in them. He said so openly. He said he didn't give a snap of his fingers for them, that he'd carry a hundred of them in his trap, if they wished. "David," said Mary Ellen, his wife, "David," she said, "you shouldn't speak like that of the good people, it will draw them on you." "Draw them be damned," he said. That very night on his way home in the trap, he was stopped by them. They took charge of the trap, they led his horse backwards and forwards all night. And while some were doing that, others got a hold of him and they danced on him, and they pounded him, and they kicked him, and they drove thorns into him, and he was that sore after it he couldn't speak for a fortnight.'

'There was a little old hag over at Nymphsfield,' said Flannery, 'and she appeared to a young fellow was going up a lane. Tucked in against the wall she was. He went over to her and he looked into her face and 'twas all wizened up. She never said a word to him, but he died two months later.'

'Well, I'll tell you of a little old woman,' said Patsy, 'and it only happened the other day, as you might say, in the time of the last war. 'Twas when the Government was putting the compulsion on a man to plough, and 'twas over at Castle Hackett it happened. And Castle Hackett is the home of all the fairies in Mayo, as every one knows. There was a field there that no man had ever ploughed. It was the field of the battle of Athenry, and in that battle there was ten thousand killed. "I don't give a damn what was fought there," said the man. "One field is the same as another," he said. But his horses were very nervous when he put them to the plough. Well, he started away to turn the sod, and he hadn't gone two furrows when a small little woman comes up to him. "What do you mean by destroying my houseen?" said she. But sure he only laughed at her. And he went on with his work, and he finished the furrow he was on, and he was half-way back on the next when the plough fell out of his hands with the pain that struck him. He lay there on the ground, and he couldn't move so much as one toe inside his boot until the neighbours came out and carried him in. With that he got the pneumonia that near killed him. His two horses were dead inside a week. His wife died, and his children were ever ailing, his crops went bad, and the plough is lying to this day half-way down the furrow, and no man will touch it.'

Mary came in at the door. She put the kettle on the fire and when it boiled we had some tea.

' 'Tis time for us to be going,' said Flannery, an hour later, making a move.

'Wait a while till I tell you what happened to my father,' said the old man.

We both sat down again.

'My father,' said he, 'was herdsman to the manor house, and one of his jobs was to boil up a good pot of mangolds and turnips every evening for the cattle. He was a very par-

ticular kind of man, and so that the roots should brew
thoroughly he not only put the iron lid on the pot, but put
a stone on the top of the lid to keep it firm. But night after
night, to his surprise in the morning, the stone was knocked
off the pot and the lid lifted. One night he said to himself,
"I'll watch," he said; and he sat up watching the pot, and
the lamp had gone down and the room was dark only for
the firelight. And what did he see but a big cat come in and
push away the stone and lift the lid off the pot, and dip his
paw into the mash just as if it was cream.

'No sooner did he see the cat than he hits it a welt of a
stick, and as it leaps through the door he puts his two dogs
after it. But the dogs were back in no time, and they shiver-
ing, as if with the fright. So he shuts the door and goes to
bed. Well, he is hardly under the sheets when the door
opens and in comes the cat that he was after hitting. And
following her, in come a dozen others, one after the other.
And they all sat down in a circle and they began to talk in
the cat language. And my father in the bed was frightened
out of his life to say a word for fear the cats would go for
him. And they all sat there mumbling and talking to each
other, when in comes the king of the cats, a great big tom
cat, he was. He walks right in, and he sits down in the
middle of them all. Then the cat that had been at the mash
limps up to him, for he was lame with the welt he was after
getting, and you'd think he was a lawyer in court the way he
spoke to the king and the others. And my father was near
dead with the fright. And the king of the cats considered for
a long while, as if he was thinking over the evidence, and
then he rose up and tapping the one that got the welt as
much as to say "Not guilty, come on," he went out of the
door. And they all followed him, and when they'd all gone
out, the door closed after them.'

'And what were they doing?' asked Flannery.

'Holding a court,' said Patsy. 'Judging my father they were. And 'twas lucky for him they judged him fair. Sure they'd have torn the eyes out of his head.'

'But did you never hear of Tim Langan,' said Mary, 'and how he was driving home one night, and the horse stopped and wouldn't go on. No matter what Tim did to him he wouldn't go on, and he was broken out all of a lather. And a big black cat came and stood before them on the road. "Will you get out of that and let us get on," said Tim. "There's no harm coming to you at all," said the cat, "if you'll take a message." "What message will I take?" said Tim. "When you get home," said the cat, "tell them Julia is wanted at the cross-roads." So Tim promised, and the cat went off and the horse trotted on as calm as you please. "What delayed ye at all?" said Tim's wife to him when he got back. "Well then, I'll tell you," said Tim. "I was stopped by the good people and the queerest thing ever happened. 'Twas a big black cat it was. 'Tell them at home,' says the cat, 'that Julia is wanted at the cross-roads.' " No sooner were the words out of his mouth than his own cat by the fire gave a start and a screech. Next minute she was out at the door with a rush and she's never been seen since.'

Once again we got up to go. There was a black cat jumped across the path as we went down the road, and a grey cat seemed to follow us up the main street of Ballinrobe.

'You'll have a little something?' said Mrs. Moran, when I reached the hotel.

'I will,' I said, 'a large one.'

CHAPTER ELEVEN

Normally one is filled with regret at the felling of a tree. We hear the crackle, the long-drawn sigh, and the crunch of a thousand branches, and we think of the infinite complexity of the growth that is now ended. Our feelings are still sad as we watch bough after bough being severed from the parent stem, as we see the limp brushwood piled high, as we see the log-laden lorry jolting its way through the rutted woodland. But at the saw-mills our feelings change. Here each baulk becomes the raw material of another existence. As each log is rolled to the bench it takes on a new life. Before our eyes there is a transformation, a resurrection. A dead tree becomes living timber. Stack after stack is piled high as it comes from the saw, quarterings, scantlings, planks; for floors, for roofs, for beds, for coffins.

At one side of Jack Moran's workshop, beside his saw-mill at Ballinrobe, cross-sections of elm branches are stacked. The bark is still on them, the moss still clings to the bark. One day they will be the stocks of cart wheels. It only needs ten minutes on the lathe. Then, for year upon year, they will revolve at the centre of their wheel, to and from field and bog, market or mass, carrying their loads of live-stock, manure, turf, or humans.

I was drawing snail shells from an island on Lough Mask when Pat Flannery called for me. No two were alike. White spiral pencillings on dark brown shells, dark brown spirals on ivory white, sometimes many bands of colour, sometimes only one, shells of pale yellow with markings of purple, shells of rose pink accented with blue.

'Would you like to see a dolmen?' said Pat. 'There's one at the top of Mile Hill.'

So we set off, and the air was heavy with the scent of gorse, and the gold of yellow-hammers' breasts was brighter than the gorse.

The dolmen was in a thicket, a few fields from the road. It was composed of the usual three great vertical slabs of stone with a capstone over them. Once they had been covered by a cairn, but the stones had recently been carted away for wall-building, and only this central chamber remained, with its ring of standing stones to mark the original boundary of the cairn. This was a good instance of a so-called 'Druid's altar' that, obviously, had never been more than a tomb. All over the country we find these megalithic remains, and again and again they are ascribed to the Druids. In actual fact they were in existence at least a thousand years before the Druids appeared in Ireland, about the fifth century B.C. It is, of course, possible that the Druids, finding these imposing structures already in being, made use of them for their own rites and ceremonies, much as Christians have converted many pagan memorials to their uses.

It is now generally believed among antiquarians that all these great monuments were built over graves, but it is still a much debated point whether or not the alignment of the stones had any relation to the rising or setting of the sun at a particular time of year such as the winter or summer solstice, or perhaps the rising or setting of some particular constellation. The late Vice-Admiral Boyle Somerville, who devoted many years to the study of this question, said: 'It requires merely the employment of a prismatic compass at a few of these ancient sites for any doubt to be dispelled.' He was of the opinion that there was very definite orientation in the plan of the stones, and an admiral with a compass is not lightly to be contradicted.

The evening was calm. We struck down across the fields to the lake, crossing the terraces of bare limestone that border its eastern shore. Across the water the hills rose lavender and grey from fields of apple green. We found the boat where we had left it a week before.

Everywhere about the lake, on rocks and on islets, gulls were sitting in pairs. On chosen sites they had begun to build, but, as yet, nests were hardly more than a few dead grasses bent to shape. There was little display among the birds, an occasional nodding of the head, otherwise they seemed content merely to be in each other's company. Only when a third bird tried to join any of the pairs was there offensive action, and that instantly.

A ringed plover was flitting from rock to rock, its move-ments the acme of precision. The bird is essentially a crea-ture of quick decisions. At one moment it is running so fast that it is hard to believe it is not flying, the next it has stopped dead, and is standing without a tremor.

Snipe rose from the rushes that edged the small islands. Many mallard were already heavy on their nests under the new green of the sally bushes, among the knife-edged boul-ders. These stones, weather-worn on shore and in the lake constantly gnawed by the acid water, are a terror to pedes-trian and boatman alike. On shore they rip one's shoe as a razor goes through soap; submerged, they pierce the plank-ings of a boat with no more trouble. It is a commonplace among botanists that in the fissures of this limestone plateau may be found a luxuriance of rare plants, a wealth that contrasts strangely with the poverty of growth existing only a few feet, or even inches, above its head. With no ex-tremes of heat or cold, no lack of moisture, shelter from the wind, and a soil constantly replenished by wind-blown dust and debris, maidenhair ferns and other delicate plants thrive as in a greenhouse.

Local history has much to say of the great fissures that exist in the limestone country, the caves that are there and the romantic legends that have become attached to many of them. It will tell you, too, of the underground streams that flow from Lough Mask to Lough Corrib, and of the great canal that was carved between the two lakes. It took years of labour in the almost solid rock. But, at last, the great day came, and Lough Mask was 'opened to the sea.'

The ceremony was a huge success, and everybody was happy until next morning when the canal was found to be dry. It has been dry ever since. The porous rock would never hold water.

It is unfortunate country, too, for trout, for many have worked their way through the fissures into pools and have been unable to return. A kindly priest told me how, in a deep hole in a rough scrubby bit of country not far from his house, he found one of these fish. 'The poor fellow was nothing but head and tail, for the want of food.' The good man had lifted a stone and found a worm under it, and this he had dropped into the pool 'and the fish came and gobbled it up.' Then he found some more and the fish gobbled those up, too. Each day afterwards he would find worms in his garden and take them along to the pool, and it delighted him to see the fish grow fat. But, at length, the term of his curacy being over, he was transferred to another parish, and no sooner had he moved than there came a man from the village with a line and a hook and on the hook he put a worm 'and he lifted the poor fish right out.'

The same priest showed me a crucifix that he had found in a cottage in his parish. It was of bog oak and was dated 1733. It was about twelve inches long, and around the crucified figure, carved in outline, were the usual emblems of the passion, ladder, spear, scourge, nails. But, in addition, there was drawn a cock standing on a pot, this in illustration of a legend widely held throughout the west of Ireland. It is told in County Mayo how the soldiers who were guarding the tomb of Christ were boiling a cock for their breakfast. Unlike the others, one of the number could not forget the rumours that he had heard. He was uneasy, and as he sat there, in the chill that precedes an eastern dawn, he said to one of his companions: 'Will he rise, d'ye think?' 'No more

than the cock in the pot,' said his fellow soldier. Then the
dawn came and with the first glint of the sun over the hills
Christ rose from the tomb, and, as he did so, the cock leaped
from the pot and crowed. And the words that he said were
'Mac-na-hoige-slán,' which being interpreted from the
Irish mean 'The Son of the Virgin is safe.'

In County Galway they say that it was Judas who, after
the betrayal, went home to find his wife cooking a cock in a
pot. He, being anxious, told his wife what he had done, saying he feared that Christ might rise. 'No more than the
cock in the pot,' said his wife, whereupon the bird leaped
out of the pot and crowed.

That evening Lough Mask was without a ripple. Land
and water were drowned in light. Save for the splashing of
mergansers in the distant creek, the water was unbroken.
We took the oars into the boat. Flannery lit his pipe. We
sat without talking, watching.

CHAPTER TWELVE

EVERYBODY SAID that I must go to Cong. Hadn't 1 stayed at Ashford Castle? they asked in surprise. Why, there wasn't the like of it in Ireland. And it wasn't so long since it was visited by royalty. 'Oh, indeed, the king himself, and no less, was over; King Edward, the old man it would be, and he in love with the place. "You like it?" said his lordship to him. 'Twas one night at dinner they were speaking. "I do, indeed," said the king. "Then 'tis yours," said his lordship. "Oh, but I couldn't do that," said the king. "Faith, it's yours," said his lordship, "from this very moment." But some of them fellows in the English Parliament wouldn't allow it. Isn't it a queer thing, as soon as a man gets into Parliament he goes to hell altogether?'

The castle was built in the nineteenth century, and, as in most of the castles of that date, the architecture is daft: false crenellations, blind machicolations, useless bartizans everywhere. But when that has been said, there is nothing left but praise, unstinted praise, for everything that a luxurious hotel should be. If any one, like Mary McMahon of County Clare, who had twenty-five husbands, one at a time, should need a permanent honeymoon address they could not do better than Ashford Castle, telephone Cong 3. There is shooting in the woods, at one time the best 'cock' shooting

in the British Isles. There is fishing in the lake. While I
was there a trout of fourteen pounds was caught. There is
history and archaeology, cairns three thousand years old,
stone circles, standing stones. There is the abbey of Cong
founded in A.D. 624. There is the church of Killarsagh,
founded by St. Fursa, the Irish saint whose visions are said
to have influenced Dante. There is the island of Inchagoill
with its church dating from the time of St. Patrick, and the
stone of Lugnaedon, the oldest Christian monument in
western Europe. The twelfth-century 'Cross of Cong,' now
in the National Museum in Dublin, is said to be the finest
piece of metal, enamel, and jewellery work of its epoch
in Europe. And there are associations with Sir William
Wilde and his son Oscar, who 'had a great brain, but made
a bad fist of himself, the poor fellow.'

Near to the cairns there may still be seen, on occasion,
'men in hundreds marching in columns and they disappearing into the ground.' On the road through the hazel
wood, not far from the big cairn where Eochy, the last king
of the Firbolgs, is said to have been buried, two men were
going home late one night. Suddenly, there appeared in
the wood 'a number of little girls and they running and
throwing lights into the trees. They all had black hair and
they were very small, and they were talking to each other,
but 'twas some sort of gibberish that no one could understand. The only thing the two men could make out was the
very last words of the girls when one of them said to the
others: "Now we have all the lamps lit," and with that they
disappeared. And no sooner were they gone than a whole
lot of men came on to the road, and one of them took a
light off of one of the trees, and he shone it up into the faces
of the other fellows, and what were they all but skeletons.
Every one was a corpse. You could see the shoulder bones

sticking through their coats and under their slouched hats was the face of death.'

Not many miles from here an old man was putting a fence round a quarry to prevent his cattle falling into it. His daughter was with him and they were renewing some of the old stakes. Near to one of the old stakes they saw a hole in the ground, and in the hole was a little iron pot, and the pot had a lid on it. They both saw it and they looked at it, and the old man took his spade and lifted the lid off it and it fell over and out of it rolled a number of gold coins. Both the old man and his daughter tried to pick up the money, but the coins ran away from them, rolling this way and that until they were all lost in the brambles and undergrowth. 'Why didn't they spit on them?' asked a listener to the story. 'Faith, they had a weakness on them when they saw all the gold,' was the reply.

CHAPTER THIRTEEN

AT FIVE O'CLOCK in the afternoon of the 16th May I sat in glory. I had pitched my tent on an island in Lough Carra, and I was surrounded by an aureole of last year's reeds, golden in decay, rising from a turquoise lake. To the west a line of distant hills might have been islands in the Aegean Sea. Pale green lights in the water suggested the shelving sands of coral lagoons. Behind me, to the south, a thick, almost impenetrable wood. To the east, beyond a haze of tall tasselled reeds, the home of my host Robert Ruttledge. He had given me the island, he had given me a boat. When I wanted food there was a chair at his table.

So I sat there, outside my tent, listening to the lapping of the water, to the cries of the gulls, to the love song of a sand-piper, 'Sissis-*see*-si sissis-*see*-si,' to the heavy beat of a pigeon's wings, to the sweetest of all music, the song of the willow wren. Overhead, there was a sky such as one glimpses through a door or window in an early Italian painting. Close by my feet a brimstone butterfly fluttered over the yellow flowers of the trefoil which broke through the grasses among the juniper and sapling birch-trees. While I watched, a mallard with her brood of youngsters swam close to the shore. Through my glasses I could see a redshank feeding on the shore of another island. It had sensed a worm in the mud. Time and again it probed, get-ting more and more excited each time. But the worm eluded it and the bird continued its peregrinations. Then, in the field beyond, a grey donkey brayed. From half a mile away a small black jackass answered. The two ran to-wards each other and, meeting, rubbed nose to nose, affectionately.

As the evening wore on I wandered into the wood. It was to me a miniature primeval world. Deep in this small jungle, creepers struggled for supremacy over a carpet of ferns, dead leaves, and nightshade. Ivy and clematis fes-tooned fallen trees, smothering branches already fleeced with moss and lichen. Everywhere a network of interlacing timbers. Deep shadows under thick holly-trees, glints of sunlight on sprays of brier.

In a glade I closed my eyes to the sudden glare of the sun. When I opened them, dazzled, the thicket seemed ablaze with stars. White flowers of strawberry, white flowers of spindle-wood, cool blue of speedwell, yellow of cinquefoil. Flowers of the blackthorn, catkins of alder. Wild thyme and sweetbrier scenting the air.

At the far side of the wood I looked through a curtain of sunlit leaves to a lake whose calm water seemed on fire. The western sky was radiant, but darkness was growing in the stones at my feet. The wind rustled in the trees, a blackbird sang, a moorhen clucked, a heron croaked. Trees grew black. Again the sandpiper's call, 'Sissis-*see*-si.' A ripple in the water brought a star to shore.

Then came night. The blackbird had ceased its singing. There seemed no sound save only from the querulous gulls. Still a faint glow in the west, but, overhead, the luminous grey of interminable space. The wind had dropped. The night air was heavy with scents. A cockchafer buzzed across the margin of the lake, a moorhen clucked again, a mouse followed the shore line, scarcely perceptible among the dark stones. Those of us born to the day must sleep at night. My bed of heaped-up rushes was waiting. As I dropped to sleep the world seemed full of crying gulls.

It is impossible to describe Lough Carra, because its aspect is ever changing. If at one moment it is burnished as a jewel, reflecting the motley of the sky, at the next there is a patina of ripples, a texture as of homespun. Unlike that of the neighbouring lakes, the bottom of Lough Carra is covered with a thick deposit of white marl, largely due, no doubt, to excess of lime in the underground springs which feed it. It is this which gives the lake its ethereal quality, a dream-like unreality.

'I suppose you haven't a crannog in the lake,' I said to my host, one evening after dinner.

'Indeed we have,' he said.

Next morning he took me to see it. Clusters of stones inside a ring of stakes were clearly visible a few feet below the surface of the water, some half-mile from the shore. We marked each stake and found that they formed a circle about thirty-three yards in diameter. But with the heavy deposit of marl it was difficult to see more than the rough outline of the structure.

'What do you think of that island down there?' he asked, pointing to a group of trees further to the south.

'It seems very neat,' I answered.

'I have often thought it is artificial,' he said.

So we rowed over to look at it.

On closer inspection there was no doubt that its almost vertical boundary wall of round stones, uniform in size, and each about as big as a man's head, could only have been built by human agency. It was quite unlike the formation of most of the other islands on the lake, which were of terraced slabs of limestone, large boulders, and quite small pebbles. We decided that a spade might give us more information.

So that afternoon we set out again, armed with spade,

fork, and billhook, and accompanied by Jim Fahy from the
farm for better service with these weapons. Ann, aged
twelve, and Veronica, aged ten, daughters of the house,
came too. They hoped that we would find a corpse. It was
as exciting as a child's adventure book.

The wind had dropped, the water was glassy calm, and
in the shallow water close to the island we could see strange
baulks of timber lying on the bottom. While Ruttledge and
I got busy on two of these, Jim began to clear a space in
the undergrowth, preparatory to digging. It took us some
little time to lever the timbers out of the encrusting marl,

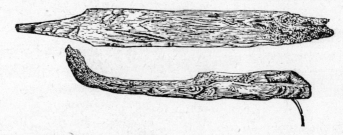

but, once into the boat, they fulfilled all expectations. One
of them was nine feet long, shouldered at one end, and
had, clearly, been worked with an adze. Its other end was
charred by fire. Its edges were bevelled. The second baulk,
which was shorter, but heavier, tapered to a 'prow' which
had also suffered from fire. As the engraving shows, there
protruded from the 'stern' a long iron nail.

But while we were admiring these discoveries there was
a shout from inside the island. 'Look what we've got,' said
Ann, producing a handful of bones. 'And these,' said Veronica, holding out some teeth and two small iron nails.
Jim had already reached a depth of four feet, where lay a
series of horizontal timbers, the foundation of the early
buildings. But that was below the present level of the lake,

and already the water was seeping in. There was little to be
seen but thick black mud. Veronica jumped into the hole
and began fingering the mud. Almost immediately she produced more teeth and bones. Being small and lissom she
could fit where no one else in the party could have gone,
and being almost double-jointed, she could squat on her
haunches with her knees behind her ears and dig in the
mud below her feet. More teeth, more bones, a fragment of
pottery came to light.

But exploration of this kind is not for the untutored.
Our duty was to inform the National Museum and send
them our specimens. In due course their report came back.
Nails, Early Christian period. Bones and teeth, mainly ox,
pig, sheep; fragments of birds, probably duck.

To build one of these crannogs must have been a tremendous undertaking. Hundreds of trees to be felled and
prepared. Hundreds of tons of stones to be ferried in
cranky canoes. It would seem that the first operation was
the erection of a circular palisade of stakes driven into the
floor of the lake. Inside the palisade horizontal logs and
brushwood were sunk, to form a foundation. Stones were
then filled in until they reached a height above the water
suitable for the erection of the house, which would be of
skilfully mortised timbers, surmounted by a thatched roof.
A pier would be built beside an opening in the palisade,
and sometimes a stone causeway would lead to the mainland. But the surface of the causeway would be below the
level of the water, and it would follow a tortuous course, so
that only those well acquainted with its plan could make
use of it. Sometimes there might be only a wooden gang-
way, easily dismantled in an emergency, to connect the
island with the shore. Thus the inhabitants were safe-
guarded alike from wild animals and human marauders.

They were not always primitive, the people who lived in these lacustrine homes. True, we have reason to believe that many of the crannogs are of very early origin, but we know also that many of them were occupied as late as the seventeenth century. Portions of harps have been found in excavated sites; finely wrought brooches, too, and combs, splendidly chased swords and scabbards, delicate drinking-cups; richly ornamented horse-trappings, beads of amber, jet, and glass set with enamel. These did not belong to an uncultured people.

Of course, Ireland isn't the only place where lake habitation has been favoured. There are well over a hundred sites of crannogs in Scotland, and the pile dwellings in the Swiss lakes are almost too well known to need mention. In Italy, Austria, and other parts of Europe, indeed all over the world, there are the remains of similar pile dwellings. Venezuela, 'Little Venice,' was given its name by the Spanish explorers when they saw the natives living in huts on piles in the water. Prescott, in his *Conquest of Mexico*, speaks of this kind of architecture as one that found great favour with the Aztecs. In East and Central Africa, in Japan, Malay, New Guinea, the same fashion reigns to-day. I remember a visit that I paid to a white man living in such a house far out in the lagoon of a Polynesian island. All the elements of romance were there, for *him*.

CHAPTER FOURTEEN

THERE IS ANOTHER ISLAND ON Lough Carra, at the northern end, Castle Island by name, so called from the thirteenth-century ruin that stands there, embedded in trees. There the hoodie crow consumes its plunder. At every step along the shore one finds empty shells, the sucked eggs of wild ducks, tame ducks, moorhens, domestic hens, turkeys, thrushes, and many others. The hoodie, or scald crow, is ubiquitous in Mayo. Everywhere he may be seen waiting, watching to make a sudden swoop on eggs or unprotected nestlings. He has his favourite sites for meals, such as the middle of a big field, out of range of guns on all sides. Castle Island is covered with trees, but its shores are a safe haunt. There are few interruptions there, at most a boat or two in the year to visit a solitary tomb and to read the inscription carved thereon:

GEORGE MOORE
Born Moore Hall 1852 Died 1933 London
He forsook his family and friends
for his art
but because he was faithful to his art
his family and friends
reclaimed his ashes for Ireland
Vale

(91)

Moore had expressed a wish to have his ashes scattered over the lake, the lake which he had watched so often as a child, the lake that 'was never out of his brain. Didn't he bring it into every one of his books? Even the Brook Kerith, that's in Palestine, sure, he compared it with the lake.'

But local feeling in County Mayo was against the idea of such 'pagan' burial. The urn was, therefore, placed in a cist cut in the solid rock of the island, and after the tomb had been sealed friends heaped over it a cairn of stones. 'Mind the wind that it doesn't blow the ashes back into the boat,' he had said to James O'Reilly, his steward.

'When he was doing a book he'd be right inside it,' said O'Reilly. 'Maybe he'd be in the middle of a conversation, and an interesting one, too, and all of a sudden he'd forget you were speaking, and he'd be a hundred miles away with his own thoughts.'

While we were speaking a dozen whimbrels, like a grey sickle, passed overhead.

'Wasn't it the queer thing that he never brought birds or wild flowers into his books?' said O'Reilly. 'He'd talk about trees, he was very fond of them, but he'd never say a word about the birds.'

It certainly was a curious thing if Moore was unconscious of the birds, for in few places could there be a lovelier daily pageant of bird life than on Lough Carra. In the deep water, crested grebe, mergansers, tufted duck; along the shores, dunlin, redshank, ringed plover, curlew, and many others, passing along this chain of lakes on their seasonal migrations, or halting a while to build their nests and rear their young. The song of the willow wren and chiffchaff is a characteristic of the wooded shores and islands. Often from my island I would see the mergansers dis-

playing. It might be one duck and two drakes. Each of the
latter, in turn, though sometimes together, would make
swift rushes through the water, splashing as he went. Then
lifting himself high in the water, balancing almost on his
tail, he would show off his salmon-tinted breast. A moment
afterwards he would rush through the water again, then,
stopping, he would thrust out his head and neck to their
farthest extent, at an angle of forty-five degrees, pull them
back quickly, and with a bowing action dip them up and
down in the water. Or it might be one drake and two ducks
swimming peaceably together until at the approach of another party the drake would commence displaying as if to
say 'Keep off.'

At other times it might be a pair of great crested grebe
facing each other, with ruff spread wide, and swaying their
heads from side to side, or perhaps, after a dive to bring up
weed, rising almost breast to breast in the water. Sometimes
it would be a pair of the less demonstrative tufted duck that
swam past with scarcely more display than an occasional
thrusting upward of the head on the part of the male, or
the repeated dipping of the bill in the water by the female.

On one island close to mine there was a mixed colony
of gulls, common and black-headed. All day long and all
night one could hear the cries of these birds, now harsh and
threatening, now soft and almost suppliant, sometimes the
sharp 'Kek—kek—kek' when, in an ecstasy of poise and
fluttering wings, the elements of a new birth were united.

On another island, but a little farther away, a pair of
greater black-backed gulls were incubating their three
eggs, the first recorded pair of these birds to nest on any
island of the lake. It would be interesting to know what
urge had driven them to choose such splendid isolation.
On the very apex of this pyramidal islet they had built.

Had they been driven from their colony by their fellows, exiled by some law of bird life, or had they, in their casual wanderings, seen this site and seen also a plentiful supply of food in the nests on the other islands?

Sandpipers were on my island, too, flitting here and there. It is curious how unlike most other wading birds they are in their lack of ceremonial immediately before mating. The male redshank, after flying in wide circles, and then up and down with quivering wings, alights beside his mate. Holding his wings aloft and fluttering them, as if to show off the delicate silver of their undersides, he utters his tremulous note. Then rising on his wings he hovers a moment before dropping to accomplish the union. The curlew, the godwit, the oyster-catcher, each has its form of address, but there seems nothing of the kind with the sandpiper. The female may be standing on a rock alone; to human observation the male may be anywhere, near or far. Suddenly he appears, and, without any preliminaries, hovers over her, flickering his wings almost as a kestrel over its hunting ground. Then, so gently, he alights on her back.

In contrast to this seemingly casual behaviour I saw two chaffinches among the blossoms on an apple-tree. Here it was obvious that the hen was expectant, fluttering, as she was, from branch to branch, sinking low and fluffing out her wings. At the moment of union she bent her head upward, and, with her bill, sweetly and tenderly caressed that of her mate throughout the seconds that the rapture lasted.

I must not forget to mention Castle Bourke, standing on the mainland at the head of the lake. Now it forms part of the outbuildings of a farm, its fragments of vaulted roofs a shelter for hens and turkeys on their nests. But many years ago the proud Bourkes lived there. Generation after generation looked out of those same narrow windows. They saw the lake as a blue mirror in summer, they saw it whitecrested under autumn squalls, they saw it whipped to milk by winter storms, they saw it amethyst and emerald in spring, to match the jewels of their brides.

'Do you think them O'Flahertys will be raiding tonight?' a lady might say. 'To hell with the O'Flahertys,' her lord would reply, as he went to look at his new litter of wolfhounds. But he might wonder to himself, as he went, at the meaning of the smoke that curled above the far hill. And she, feeling that all was safe, would wander by the lake, perhaps to gather leaves of the butterwort for her dairy—warm milk poured over them will solidify into a light cheese—or she may have gone to seek plantain leaves, as a salve for wounds, or the common daisy that helps bones to knit, or the lesser celandine that preserves the teeth. She might have gone merely to gather a posy. Knowing that to pick the fly-orchids which carpet the marshy ground in May would weaken the plants she would leave them to grow, but the blue flowers of the milkwort and the crimson and gold of the vetches, blended with fronds of the wild maidenhair fern, would fit the old horn drinking-cup propped up on the table by her window.

CHAPTER FIFTEEN

FROM LOUGH CARRA I went to Inishbofin, 'Island of the White Cow,' some four miles off the coast of County Galway. Its name is derived from a legend that tells how, once upon a time, the island was spectral, wrapped in mist, appearing and disappearing. One day some fishermen, lost in a fog, came close to its shore. Landing, they lit a fire, or, as some say, one of them knocked the ashes from his pipe. Anyway, the moment that fire touched the soil the enchantment was broken. The island became fixed, the mist cleared away, and the fishermen found themselves on what is now known as North Beach, a long bank of shingle separating the sea from an inland lake. As they looked around them they saw an old woman driving a white cow towards the lake. The moment it touched the water she struck it, whereupon it was turned into stone. One of the men, then, being indignant at the behaviour of the old woman, struck her, whereupon both he and she were turned into stone. It is said that those rocks are still there for all to see, in proof of the story. But for some reason, perhaps another enchantment, I was unable to find them.

There was no particular reason why I should visit Bofin except that a casual acquaintance in Clifden had told me that I ought to go there. The day I went I met the local doctor on the pier. 'Hallo, Bob!' he said. Although we had never met he knew the sister-in-law of a cousin of mine. Of course I must come back. Anything he could do for me he would do for me, he said. All I had to do was send him a card giving the approximate date of my arrival, and he would make all arrangements at the hotel. He said 'approximate' because the journey depended largely on the weather.

As things turned out I was storm-bound for four days on my next attempt to reach the island. But it is no hardship to stay at Clifden, the nearest town to the port of Cleggan. There are comfortable hotels there. Everybody knows everybody, and all about everybody, and the days slip by. Besides, I could go inland among the purple mountains of Connemara, I could go south along the coast, following crescent after crescent of silver-sanded bays; bays where men from wrecked ships of the Spanish Armada once struggled ashore, bays where many a cask has been landed on a dark night, bays where one may find large, mahogany-coloured beans, seeds of giant tropical climbing plants, that have drifted across four thousand miles of ocean from South America and the West Indies. Many of them may be made to germinate in a greenhouse even after more than a year in the salt water.

Along that shore too the sea-pies congregate and the ringed plovers nest. One of these birds in her anxiety to

lead me from her eggs actually disclosed them to me. At
the time I was meditating on the sand-hoppers, just then
lying so quiet under the tide-strewn weed, but who, an
hour after sunset, would be leaping and dancing from
mud to stone, from stone to mud, pattering and clattering
on the sand like hailstones on an iron roof. Had the bird
remained on her nest, I should have passed, unseeing. As
it was, my thoughts were distracted by a low chattering
cry, and looking in the direction whence it came I saw her
flat on a rock, with her wings fluffed out, flapping, seemingly helplessly. I knew her game but I joined in it, following where she led me. Even so on my way back I saw
the nest with its four grey spotted eggs only a few feet
above high-water mark and decorated, as usual, with fragments of shell and small stones.

To many people it must, at first thought, seem strange
that the great majority of birds' eggs have their markings
heaviest towards their blunt end. But the reason becomes
clear when it is known that most, if not all, eggs are laid
blunt end first. In their passage down the oviduct it is this
area of greatest diameter which exerts the greatest pressure
against the walls of the oviduct, wherein are situated the
pigmentary papillae. Hence it is that area which absorbs
the greater part of the colouring matter. In cases where the
egg has remained stationary for a while the edges of the
markings are clearly defined. Where the egg has moved
before the colour has set there are blurred edges. A rotary
movement of the egg causes such veinings as we see on the
eggs of the yellow-hammer and other buntings.

It was a day of heavy showers, and during one of them I
stepped inside a cottage for shelter. The old man was sitting by a wooden trough mashing potatoes for his pigs. His

wife had a broom in her hands with which she swept out
the rain that blew in under the front door.

'Why the divil she must be using that door to the south,
when there's another one there to the north, I don't know,'
said the old man. 'Why couldn't she block it up and we'd
be having a dry floor?'

'Ah, but I like to see the motors passing,' said the old
woman.

'Would there be many coming along here?' I asked, for
it was a side road and out of the way.

'Indeed there would,' she said. 'I declare to God you'd
see one every day.'

After four days in Clifden the *Lady of Lourdes* arrived
in Cleggan harbour, with the doctor from Bofin on board.
He had come in merely for the trip. He likes rough
weather. The only passengers, besides ourselves, on the
return journey were two young pigs. They lay in a sack
on the floor of the open cockpit.

As we left the pier we could see line beyond line of
breaking waves ahead of us. One moment the sea was
bright green, the next it was deep purple, the next steel
grey or inky black. Out of the shelter of the land we
lurched and we pitched, we pirouetted and we gyrated.
Gannets were diving. Guillemots were rising and falling
with each wave. Spray came over us. Sometimes it was more

than spray. There was nowhere to sit. We just stood and held on to the nearest rope or timber.

The island of Bofin is four miles long and two miles wide. It is deeply indented, not only by welcoming bays, but by inhospitable chasms. Inland on the high ground one is conscious mostly of rocky, boulder-strewn escarpments, with intervening patches of shallow bog. At the lower levels and close to the shore, white cottages dot the landscape. Some are roofed with slates, others with thatch, but the thatch needs a network of straw ropes weighted with stones to resist the gales. On the open beaches, in fine weather, curraghs may be seen lying bottom uppermost. In stormy weather their owners lift them behind the protecting walls of fields.

The Bofin curragh differs from those of the Aran Isles in that there are no spaces between the timbers. A close framework of wood covers the ribs before the canvas is applied. On the Arans the framework is open, a mere skeleton. For the most part nothing but tarred canvas separates the voyager from a long deep dive.

Since the twelfth century Bofin has had many owners. The O'Flahertys, the O'Malleys, the Duke of Lorraine, the Cromwellians, the Jacobites, the Williamites, the Clanricardes have all had their turn. To-day the Congested Districts Board directs its fortunes. At the beginning of the last century its population and that of the neighbouring island of Inishshark were together about fourteen hundred souls, but to-day it is little more than half that. Many of the names show a Norman origin, such as D'Arcy, de Courcy, de Lacy, Lavelle, Prendergast, but there are plenty of old Irish stock as well. There is music in such place-names as Alladoon, Bunamullen, Cooltra, Mweelanbwee, Ooghnagunnel, Cloonamore.

After the Synod of Whitby in A.D. 664, at which a controversy had raged about the rule for the keeping of Easter,
St. Colman, then Abbot of Lindisfarne, left that monastery, taking with him all the Irish and thirty of the English
monks. At first they settled on the island of Iona, but later
came to Inishbofin and founded a monastery there. For a
while all went well, and tradition says that hundreds of
students flocked to Bofin not only to imbibe learning but
also to learn the arts of calligraphy and illumination, as
taught by the disciples of St. Columcille. His was the school
that produced the Book of Kells, the Book of Durrow, the
Book of Lindisfarne, and other glories of Irish art which,
among all the illuminated manuscripts of the world, have
never been surpassed.

But 'eventually,' I was told, 'they didn't get on at all
together, for the Irish fellows would be out with the gun,
hunting and shooting all day, while the English fellows
would be at home in the garden, digging the spuds and
the rest, and there was a great falling out between them.
So when St. Colman seen that, " 'Tis better for you," he
says to the Englishmen, " 'tis better for you go over to
County Mayo. Do as I tell you, now," he said, "and I'll
come with you myself," he said. And sure they did great
things over there.'

The fact that gunpowder was not invented until six hundred years after the saint had led his English followers to
County Mayo does not affect the main truth of the story
that there was then, as now, a difference in temperament
between men of the two nations.

The monastery building was never large. To-day it is
nothing more than two gable ends and their side walls,
set deep in nettles. It is surrounded by graves whose only
'headstones' are the staves, like broken oars, on which the

coffins had been carried, graves edged with white pebbles and covered with sea shells. Thousands of shells of lowly creatures to mark the remains of one individual a little higher in the scale.

In a fragment of a skull that lay in the crevice of a wall a blackbird had built its nest. It seemed to me a happy thought that, when all our loves and pains are over and the tired old brain has gone back to earth, perhaps, from the most unmusical of us all, blackbirds may sit in the hollies and sing the spring day through.

CHAPTER SIXTEEN

I MENTIONED SUCH NAMES as Alladoon, Bunamullen, Cooltra, Mweelanbwee, names lovely in themselves, but even more lovely when a little of their significance is understood. *Alla* a cliff, *doon* a fort; Alladoon, the Cliff of the Fort: *bun* the end of anything, *mullen* a hillock; Bunamullen, the Foot of the Hillock: *cool* back, *tra* a strand; Cooltra, Back Strand: *mweelan* summit or ridge, *bwee* yellow; Mweelanbwee, Yellow Ridge. It is so with almost all the names throughout the country, and I know of no more romantic book than Dr. Joyce's study of *The Origin and History of Irish Names of Places*. Of course, a number of the names, as we know them to-day, have departed far from their original forms. Even so, it is possible, with but a few words of Irish, to interpret the meaning of many others and find much that sheds light on past history.

There are over six thousand places in Ireland whose name begins with the word *Bally,* from *baile,* a town. There are about fourteen hundred townlands or villages in Ireland whose name begins with the word *Lis;* there are about half that number beginning with *Dun,* and as many with *Rath,* all three words signifying fortifications of one kind or another: Lismore, the Great Fort; Dundalk, formerly Dun-Dealgan, the Fort of Delga; Rathdrum, the Fort of the Druim, or hill-ridge.

(103)

Cnoc, pronounced 'knock,' with its diminutives *knockane, knockaun, knockeen,* gives us such places as Bally-knockane, the Town of the Little Hill; and Knockaun-eevin, the beautiful Little Hill. From the appearance at dawn of Knockfierna, in County Limerick, the local people can predict the weather; hence its name, the Hill of Truth, meaning of truthful prediction. Knocknaloori-caun, in County Waterford, means the Hill of the Cluri-cauns (*cluricaun,* like leprechaun, a kind of fairy). *Sidh,* pronounced 'shee,' was the name originally given to the fairies' palaces; later the word came to denote the hills in which the palaces were situated; finally it was, and is still, applied to the fairies themselves. Sheerim, the old name for the Rock of Cashel, meant Fairy-ridge. Cloonshee means Fairy-meadow; Ballynasheoge, the Town of the Little Fairies; Knocknasheega, the Hill of the Fairies. *Cill,* a church, became anglicized to *kil, kyle, keel,* or *cal.*

Joyce has many other interesting facts to give us. For instance, he tells of the three sons of Erc, by name Fergus, Angus, and Loarn, who, in A.D. 506, crossed over to Scotland and colonized that part of the country now known as Argyllshire, that name signifying Airer-Gaedhil ('arrer-gale') the territory of the Gael, or Irish. He tells, too, how some five hundred years later, 'by one of the most curious instances on record,' the name of one country became transferred to another. He writes: 'The name Scotia originally belonged to Ireland, and the Irish were called Scoti or Scots; Scotland, which was anciently called Alba, subsequently got the name of Scotia minor, as being peopled by Scots from Ireland, while the parent country was for distinction often called Scotia major. This continued down to about the eleventh century, when Ireland returned to the native name *Eire,* and Scotia was thenceforward exclusively applied to Scotland.' The word 'land' was in both cases added later.

The Irish for water is *uisce,* and it occurs frequently in place-names, Knockaniska, Killisky, etc. But it also occurs in the word *uisce-beatha,* which becomes anglicized to *usquebaugh,* and, slightly altered, now passes as an English word, whisky. Literally, like the Latin *aqua-vitae* and the French *eau-de-vie, usquebaugh* means 'water of life.'

Many other words connected with water occur again and again, but none more often than *tobar,* a well, with its variants *tober, tipper, tubbrid.* In Ireland, as in almost every other country, wells have been held sacred from the earliest times. Scarcely a village that has not its well where illness may be cured, or intercession obtained. At one time the worship of these wells was 'elemental,' but to-day the pools are dedicated to Christian saints, though traces of the earlier faith still remain. They linger, too, in other countries. Miss Gordon Cumming tells of a young man in Scotland who was seen to kneel at a well and take a draught, after which he rose and said: 'O Lord, Thou knowest that weel would it be for me this day an' I had stoopit my knees and my heart before Thee in spirit and in truth as often as I have stoopit them afore this well. But we maun keep the custom of our fathers.' Not very long ago, on a lonely moor in Aberdeenshire, women were seen dancing in a circle, with hands joined, round the well of Melshach. Their garments were fastened high up under their arms, and an aged crone who sat in their midst dipped a small vessel into the well and sprinkled them with the water. So did they hope to induce fruitfulness. Primitive man saw in water its power of bestowing fertility on his fields, and venerated it accordingly. It was to him the expression of a living force, a force or spirit that had to be appeased or propitiated. To-day, in parts of Rumania, a woman drawing water will pour back a few drops as an offering to the spirit of the well. At Sūs, in Morocco, there is a miracle-working spring. Every year, on 8th October, two cows, big with calf, are slaughtered on the bank. They are killed in such a way that their blood flows into the water. It is believed that if this sacrifice were omitted the crops would fail. Even in Palestine almost every spring has its guardian spirit, and few peasant women will let down their bucket without a word of propitiation.

In many places it is customary to approach the wells 'sunwise,' even as funerals may sometimes be seen to approach the cemetery. Perhaps this is in honour of another life force, the sun, which we more sophisticated folk also propitiate when we pass the wine, when we dance, even when we play cards.

CHAPTER SEVENTEEN

THERE HAD BEEN STORMS for a week, so that any communication between Bofin and the mainland had been impossible. The priest was away from the island, in hospital after an accident. The doctor and I sat in his house. We hoped to distract our thoughts with his wireless, but the battery had run down and transmission was bad. If we got the beginning of a sentence we missed the end of it, if we got the end there had been no beginning. From the window we could see line beyond line of breakers, a million crests of waves. The wind roared in the chimney, large gouts of rain struck the windows. For a moment the sun would gleam on the crimson fuchsia hedge outside the door, for a moment glints of gold would strike the distant hill where stood the fort of Grania. Through a break in the mist Don Bosco, the Spaniard's Castle, at the mouth of the harbour, would tell purple against a milk-white sea; then sky and sea would be merged again in driving rain.

The doctor recited from Thomas Hood:

'. . . No travelling at all—no locomotion,
No inkling of the way—no notion—
    "No go"—by land or ocean—
    No mail—no post—
No news from any foreign coast—'

(107)

'It was a day like this in February, only worse,' he said, 'when little Kathleen, over at West Quarter, developed acute appendicitis. We had to get her to the mainland for an operation. But the mail boat wasn't running. No boat was running. We would lose her if we didn't get her across. So I went along to Michael Scuffle. He was there in the cottage, with his three nephews, when I went in. The boys were mending nets, and Michael was whittling an oar. "Michael," I said, "we must get that child to hospital." Michael put the oar out of his hand and turned to the boys. "Will you come?" he said. That was all he said: "Will you come?" The boys said nothing. They just got up and put on their oilskins. We went down to the boat and I took the child in my arms and they wrapped a sail around the two of us. The child fell asleep when she felt the motion of the boat. It took us four hours to do the one-hour journey, with green water breaking over us all the way. But she's well and strong to-day.'

From the window we could see the surf leaping high over the battered sea wall. An occasional dark figure battled its way against the storm.

'But we're better off than they are on Turk,' continued the doctor. 'They may be cut off there for three months on end, without priest or doctor. If a man dies he dies, and he is buried, and the priest reads the funeral service over him when next he visits the island, maybe a month or more later. At the best of times it takes a boat half a day to beat up from the mainland against the prevailing wind. And Shark, across the way, isn't much better. Mass once a month. For three weeks last winter they couldn't move from the island.'

Even during the finest weather there is danger of sudden storms. Not many years ago, on 'the calmest night of the week,' a gale hit the fishing boats, and few of them reached land. Forty-four men lost their lives. Pat Concannon, on Bofin, still has the marks on his hands of the rope that he held for seven hours that night, the rope that, fastened to his net as a sea-anchor, kept the head of his boat to the wind. There had been a warning on the wireless from Daventry, but it had been missed on the island. Local weather experts saw no sign of coming storm. Only one incident gave cause for anxiety. A few nights earlier a phantom ship had been seen. It had followed the boats all through the night. It had made no answer to any of the hails from the boats. This the men took as a warning. But they could not give up their means of livelihood.

The night of the storm there were boats from Cleggan and Rossadilisk on the mainland fishing with those from Bofin. The gale came on them suddenly, so suddenly that there was no time to cut away the nets. In the darkness men still in the boats could hear the shouts of their friends drowning. One man saw his brother go down within an oar's length of him but could do nothing to help.

For seven hours Pat held the rope, his knees wedged against the stem post of the boat. Up each wave he had to haul her lest she should broach to, then he would slack away the rope to let her down the other side. Occasionally he would shout orders to the younger members of the crew. All the time the sea was rising, angered by the ebb-tide against the wind. The blow had started at seven o'clock in the evening. By two o'clock in the morning they had drifted nine miles, and now they were in danger of running on the breakers off High Island. But the wind had begun to drop, so they cut their nets and made for Cleggan. It took them two hours of desperate rowing to get there. When they reached land they found the bodies of many of their friends already washed ashore, some of them tangled in their own nets.

It is the custom in the west, when the men are fishing, for the women of the house either to stay awake in bed or to remain dressed about the house in order to keep the fire going. That night nobody on shore had lain down. When Pat Concannon and his crew landed Pat walked up to the house of a friend. 'Good night, Mrs. King,' he said.

'Good night, Pat,' she said. 'What has you here at this hour of the night?' 'I was waiting round,' he said, 'and I thought I'd come in and sit down by the fire.' Mrs. King made him a cup of tea. Later the doctor came and dressed his hands. Nothing more was said. 'The grief was too great.'

CHAPTER EIGHTEEN

INISHBOFIN HAS TWO neighbouring islands, Inishturk and Inishshark. Inishturk, which I was unable to reach owing to bad weather, lies five miles to the north of Bofin. Its name signifies 'Island of the Wild Boar.' Inishshark, on the west, is but a mile away at its nearest point, though from pier to pier it is more than double that distance. The meaning of its name is somewhat obscure, some authorities suggesting that it is called after Earc, a pre-Christian hero.

On Shark they are envious of the people of Bofin. I was told there that you could get everything on Bofin that you could get on the mainland. 'There's a shop there, there's a post office there, they have a priest and a doctor, and what more could any man want?'

There are no police on these islands. Any disagreements are settled among the people themselves. Nor are the police encouraged to visit the islands. 'What do they want there but to be making trouble?' Anyway, the mail boat is only under contract to carry mails. There is no obligation to carry visitors, particularly those in uniform. But some-how or other, a little while ago, a member of the Civic Guard did manage to reach Bofin. He even went so far as to arrest a poor unsuspecting islander and proceed to take him to the mainland. He got his man to the boat and he got his boat away from the pier and he congratulated him-self on the tactful way in which he had handled a difficult situation.

There are two ways out of the harbour; one, the more usual, broad and open to the sea. The other, a shorter route, only possible at certain tides, a narrow channel close to the rocky headland on which stands Don Bosco's castle. On this occasion, to save time, for the evening was getting late, the helmsman chose the shorter route, and, probably to escape some hidden danger, he took the course particu-larly fine. With one jump the prisoner was ashore. 'Good-bye to you now,' he called as he legged it up the rocks behind the castle. It was an affair of a moment. Another landing was impossible. There was no room in that nar-row channel for manœuvre. There was no room even to go about. The only course was out into the open sea and then back by the main channel, beating up against the westerly wind. For some reason, that day, the wind was

very contrary and the boat difficult to handle. More than
once she 'missed stays' and got into 'irons,' that is to say,
she stuck with her head in the wind and her sails flapping,
refusing to move one way or the other without the use of
an oar. And somehow the oars had got tangled in some
ropes.

By the time that officer was back in harbour and ashore
his victim was in a curragh heading from the other side of
the island for the mainland of Mayo. It was a weary and
seasick constable that reached the coast of Galway that evening, many hours after dark.

Don Bosco, who 'reigned for three generations,' lives in
tradition as a man of large stature, a corsair on the ocean,
but of strictly fair dealings at home. From his castle on the
southern headland of the island he had a chain-boom across
the harbour which he defended for a fortnight against
twenty-two ships of the line. But in 1652 he capitulated to
the forces of the Commonwealth, whose record here is no
better than elsewhere. As Macaulay wrote: 'Cromwell gave
free rein to the fierce enthusiasm of his followers and they,
waging war resembling that which Israel waged on the
Canaanites, smote idolaters with the edge of the sword.'
That was his policy on Bofin and there is a tradition there
of a massacre as bloody as that of Glencoe.

The ruined castle is now frequented by cattle, who find
there a sheltered spot to await their milking. The roofless
walls resound to the cries of choughs and overhead the
white terns circle. With the falling tide the rocks below
are fringed with emerald weed, and in the sheltered water
the long brown blades of oar-weed push their heads above
the surface and sink away again like seals at play.

'There's that seal in the harbour again,' said Pat Concannon one day, 'and he always brings bad weather.'

'For God's sake will you drive him out!' said the doctor.

But it wasn't always bad weather. Sometimes there would be days of high fine flecks of cloud and dazzling sunlit water. Sometimes there would be grey days with light winds from the west. Then we would go fishing. A dull sultry evening with thunder in the air is the best for pollack. It might be for part of a day with Pat Concannon in his pookawn, or it might be for a night and a day with Michael Scuffle in his trawler. The pookawn is an open boat about twenty feet long. It carries a single sail, a lug, from bow to stern. Pat's pookawn was comparatively new. On Bofin men do not go to sea a second time in boats that have seen disaster. A boat which has lost a man is not used again. It will be left to rot, or for the tide to carry away. It is believed that a good boat-builder will know when repairing a boat whether or not it is a lucky one. 'She's a good boat and a sound boat, but sell her,' was the advice given recently. But the owner heeded not the advice, and disaster followed.

White stones are unlucky, especially in a boat. No fisherman on the west coast will take them as ballast. 'Them's no good.' 'Them's unlucky.' 'Hens lay them.' I heard a man trying to persuade the priest that it was a white stone that had thrown him from his bicycle. The priest did not think so, but the man, who was not present at the accident, was convinced of it. Whatever the origin of the belief may be, the association of white pebbles with the dead goes back a very long way, for we find these stones a constantly recurring feature in bronze age burials, placed beside the cremated remains. The belief in their magic power is not confined to Ireland. In Strathnaver, in Scotland, 'an old woman did many marvellous things by means of a white pebble.' In Sandsting parish in the Shetlands a quartz pebble about the size of an egg was used to cure sterility. The stone was placed in running water and the would-be mother washed her feet in water drawn from the stream.

The association of these stones with hens again connects with ill luck, for hens' eggs buried in a neighbour's field will bring misfortune on the owner of that land. Hens themselves can be unlucky, too. I know of people in County Galway who will on no account carry a hen in their car, unless it be a bird being taken to market. Such a thing as a hatching hen to a friend cannot be managed. A furred animal must never be mentioned to a man going fishing, in particular a fox. If you want to make a Connaught fisherman fighting mad, call 'Sionnac,' that is the Irish for fox, at him as he goes to his boat. In a moment of annoyance a fisherman from Bofin shouted the word 'Cat' at another in the boat with him. 'Up with the lines,' said the skipper, 'we're going home.' But they persuaded him to change his mind and, in spite of the imprecation, they caught sixteen hundred bream.

But, avoiding such complications, it is grand to feel the tiller against your ribs and the main sheet tugging in your hand, with the stern quarter awash and spray coming over forrard, and the boat leaping and bouncing, and a silver wake of rustling water astern.

The doctor is hauling in a fish. Pat is telling us a story. 'Why do you talk so fast?' says the doctor.

'What else would you do in a boat?' is the answer. In the face of the Atlantic there is no time for slow thoughts or drawling speech.

The spray strikes one's eyes. It is salt on one's lips. The water around is black. White flecks of foam pass to leeward. We dip into a trough and almost lose way as we rise to the next wave. The doctor and Pat are hauling. Both are good fish. Pollack, five or six pounds each. The sail flaps. I let her head away and again she is sailing. All the time watching the luff of the sail, watching to see that it is filled. By that I know if she is 'sailing.' Curious that now the mast scarcely enters my consciousness, yet, later, when I lie down to sleep, it will not be the filling or flagging of the sail that is uppermost in my mind, but rather the swinging to and fro of that masthead against the flecks of passing cloud. So, it would seem, are we influenced not so much by those things of which we are most conscious, but by those things on which our conscious thoughts depend, the masts that hold the sails.

They have a simple but effective form of weather-glass on Bofin. It consists of a jam jar with about an inch of water at the bottom. In this, supported by a ring of cork, stands, inverted, a small empty flask, something like a miniature of those used for Chianti. Many of them are said to have been washed ashore on the island. The mouth of the flask is just below the level of the water. As with our mercury barometers the water rises in the neck of the flask for fine weather and, correspondingly, falls at the approach of storms.

CHAPTER NINETEEN

'GIVE ME A CIGARETTE, doctor,' said Michael Scuffle, coming in at the door of the hotel sitting-room one evening about six o'clock. 'Will the two of ye come fishing?' he added.

Michael stands over six feet high, his hips are lean, his shoulders broad. His eyes shine blue from a face deep tanned by the weather.

'There's nothing ye want. Come as ye are. We've plenty on board,' he said.

So ten minutes later we had climbed out of his punt on to the deck of the *Ave Maria*, where his nephews Patrick and Edward greeted us. Another ten minutes and the engine had started, the punt was left swinging on the moorings, and we were heading away to the fishing grounds, four miles to the south. Outside the harbour flocks of guillemots, ten and twenty at a time, shot by, flying south. An occasional puffin flew in the same direction.

We passed through a shoal of basking sharks, many of them twenty or thirty feet long, a few even longer. Locally, and off the coast of Wales, they are known as sun-fish, from their habit of lying near the surface of the water in warm weather. For the most part they are inoffensive to man, feeding like the whalebone whales on the minute creatures, shrimp-like and otherwise, known as plankton. Even

so, a flick from their tail would make matchwood of an
ordinary small boat, and the helmsman is wise who steers
his course accordingly. The true sun-fish, sometimes called
the head-fish from its truncated appearance, is also a visitor
to our coasts in summer. It does not, as a rule, exceed a
length of ten feet, but, being almost as deep as it is long,
it may weigh a ton. Sometimes solitary or in pairs, sometimes in small schools, numbering a dozen or more, it also
likes to idle near the surface, its high dorsal fin, like shining
metal, above the surface.

There was scarcely a breath of wind as we moved along.
Wide areas of smooth, seemingly burnished, water alter-
nated with streaks shot like silk, stippled by passing whiffs
of air. Patrick was standing astern, with the tiller between
his legs. His hands were in his trouser pockets. His cap
was on the back of his head, peak astern. He was wearing
high sea boots. A blue jersey, 'gansey' they call it, fitted
tight to his waist. He said little, but whenever we looked
in his direction there was a quiet smile on his face. Michael
and Edward were busy spreading the trawl along the deck.
Sometimes Michael would give directions. Most of the
time Edward was singing. If he stopped singing it was because he wanted to laugh, his laugh an infectious chuckle.

When the net itself was ready, an otter board, weighing
nearly a hundredweight, was put against the gunwale
abreast of the mast, another was balanced across the stern.
These weighted boards are so attached to the net that they
fan out and keep the mouth of the net not only wide open,
but close to the sea floor. Two coils of rope each of sixty
fathoms, connecting the otter boards with our boat, lay on
deck, on either side of the mast.

But there was time before the trawl was shot. We passed
the Cuddoo rocks with the long swell breaking on them.

We saw the cottages on the mainland, shining white and gold, and the hills behind them rose-tinted in the evening light. The sea was indigo blue. We passed boats which had reached the grounds before us, and were now moving slowly under the strain of their trawls.

Then Michael gave the word. Patrick, at the tiller, took a step to port, our bow swung to starboard, and, as it did so, Michael and Edward shot the trawl over the starboard side. First the purse, the strongly netted bag at the end, into which the catch eventually finds its way; then as quickly as possible the wings that guide the fish towards the purse, then the otter boards; finally fathom after fathom from the two coils of rope. By swinging the boat sharply, at the moment of shooting, the net had gone over 'broadside' and fanned out immediately, clear of all possible entanglements.

Gulls now appeared astern, the herring gull with its golden bill, the kittiwake so delicate in build, so buoyant in its flight. An occasional guillemot bobbed up and down beside us.

Our speed slackened as the trawl pulled. Michael lit a cigarette. Edward and the doctor went below to the galley. Edward began a snatch from *Galway Bay*:

'To see again the ripple on the trout stream,
    The women in the meadows making hay,
  To sit beside a turf fire in a cabin
    And to watch the bare-foot gossoons at their play.'

Before he could tell us any more, a shout from Michael brought him on deck. The engine was churning up the water astern and we were no longer moving. The net was foul. Everybody sprang into action. The engine was put into reverse, and then out of gear. And the haul began. This is the time you'd know there were sixty fathoms. Paddy was on one rope. Michael and Edward were together on the other. Yard after yard, yard after yard, then foot after foot, straining at the ropes, they made full use of the rise and fall of the ship. As the stern lifted on a wave they held fast, then as it sank into a trough and the rope eased in their hands they heaved. At last, the otter boards appeared, sidling here, sidling there in the water, white, like great skate. They were lifted on board. Then came the wings of the net, from which a scarlet gurnard dropped, fantastic apparition from another world, shimmering on the deck, sharp spines erect, spined fins spread taught, flashing all reds; yet lost, utterly lost on the grey wooden deck, where no water was, only air, a thing unknown. A sole and two brill followed, helplessly flapping.

The net was clear, only one small tear, soon mended. We were moving to cleaner ground. Edward and the doctor were again in the foc's'le and Edward was singing. This time it was *The Queen of Connemara*:

'. . . When the dark flood of the ocean and the white foam
    rush together
High she rides, in her pride, like a sea-gull thro' the gale.'

And the doctor would join him in the chorus:

'Oh she's neat, Oh she's sweet; she's a beauty every line,
The *Queen of Connemara*, that bounding barque of mine.'

The sun had dropped in a cloudless sky. One last glimpse of the blazing arc as we rose on a swell. Then crimson and lilac in the west, with the white foam on the rocks turned to lavender. Tea came up from below in a saucepan, with slabs of home-made bread. The butter had gone soft in the heat of the galley so we put it into a bucket of sea-water and waited while it hardened.

Gradually the brighter colours left the sky. Passing boats became silhouettes. Rocks grew blacker than ever. The evening star dropped, deep red, below the horizon.

So, into the silver night, with phosphorus glinting at our bows and shining from our trawl ropes. Slowly, so slowly, we moved forward, rising and falling, and rolling. Paddy still stood at the helm, dark against the sky, like some heroic figure of the past. 'You couldn't buy a night like this,' said Michael.

All around was silver, save for the rocks that loomed to east and west, breaking the surface like seals and whales at play. 'Did you ever hear the story of the seals on Clare Island?' I asked Michael.

'I did not,' he said.

So I told him how three men had gone seal-hunting one day, and how one of them had landed in one cave while the other two went further to search in another. The sea got up while they were away so that when they came back they were unable to take the first man off. 'Go home,' he called to them, 'and come back for me in the morning, for there's a fine bench of a rock here that I can sleep on.' So they went away and they left him, and he lay down to sleep for there was nothing else for him to do. And after he'd been asleep for a while he was wakened by the sound of great splashing, and in the half light that was in the cave he could see a big herd of seals. No sooner had they come up on the shingle in the cave than they took off their skin coats, and underneath they were nothing but ordinary men and women. And the men lay down and went to sleep near the water, and the women lay down higher up where the stones were drier, and one of them was quite close to where the fisherman lay. So they slept there all night, but in the first light of morning, before ever the seals woke up, the fisher-

man put out his hand and caught a hold of the skin coat of
the woman that was near him, and he pulled it up to him
and hid it under him where he was lying. And one by one
the seals woke up and put on their coats of fur and swam
away out to sea, until there was only the one left, the
woman whose coat the fisherman had hidden. And she was
screeching at the other seals not to leave her. But they did,
and she was there, and she couldn't go out to sea without
the fur, and she was a fine handsome woman. So the fisherman spoke kindly to her, and when the boat came back for
him she went with him, and they got married, and she had
two children by him. And they were happy enough until
one day their house caught fire and the woman got the
smell of burning fur from the skin that her husband had
left hidden up in the rafters. With that she made a jump
at it, and got a hold of it, and away to the sea with her, and
only once was she seen again after, and that was when she
came back, one evening, to kiss her children when they
were playing by the shore.

'That's all nonsense,' said Michael.

'And,' I said, 'another time some men from Clare Island
went out beyond Achill Head looking for seals, and they
found three of them in a cave and they struck at them with
their clubs and they hit each one of them three times. But,
in spite of the heavy blows, the seals got away to the sea.
So the men got into their curragh to look for more seals.
But no sooner were they at sea than a storm came up and
they were blown out of sight of all land, and they didn't
know where they were and they were sure they'd be
drowned. But just when they'd given up their last hope
they saw a light and they pulled for it, and they found
themselves on an island they'd never seen before, and there
was a cottage there. So they went up to the cottage and

there was a woman there making plasters for three men who were stretched on the floor with terribly ugly wounds on their backs. "What in the world happened to you?" asked one of the visitors. " 'Tis you surely should know what happened to us," said one of the men on the floor, "for 'tis you yourselves and none others that's after striking us, east in the cave at Achill." "And what will we do now?" said the visitors, for they were in a great fright. "Do nothing at all," said the men on the floor, "only leave seals alone in the future." So they promised them that, and the storm went down, and one of the seal-men showed them the way they should go home, and they never again touched a seal.'

'You wouldn't believe that!' said Michael. The men of Bofin, to-day, have little inclination for stories.

The glow in the north-western sky was gradually moving to the north. It was close on midnight. 'We'll haul,' said Michael.

Again the sixty fathoms of ropes, arm over arm, arm over arm. This time the net was well filled. It was too heavy to lift on board without the block and tackle. Once on board, Michael untied the codstring and the deck became alive with struggling fish. They slithered on one another. They flapped, they gasped. The rays lashed their long tails. Dark crabs crept away and hid in the scuppers. A cod gaped and gaped and gaped. A starfish lay motionless. Plaice, brill, whiting, gurnard, haddock everywhere.

The trawl was shot again. Eddy, having helped to clear the deck of undesirables such as dogfish, sea-urchins, and spider-crabs, joined the doctor in the galley. The doctor was already filleting a brill with his penknife. Eddy stoked the stove with turf. Every now and again his rippling laugh would break the silence.

We seemed to be aloof from the whole world, alone in a vast sphere of silver light. Then, to the south, we glimpsed another boat passing. 'It's nice to have company,' said Michael. ' 'Tis lonesome never to see a boat.'

The doctor appeared from the galley carrying the cooked brill on brown paper. It had been fried in butter. The roof of the hatch served as table. Eddy brought more tea. No two cooks ever served a better meal.

'There's no night,' said Michael. Although it was less than an hour after midnight, warm tints were already creeping into the northern sky. One by one the stars went out and the grey turned to copper. But it was two hours more before the sun lipped the horizon. Meanwhile they had hauled again. Little in it that time but long strands of crinkled wrack, thongs and flattened fronds of dark brown slippery weed.

And so, for me, to sleep, on a coil of rope in the bow. When I woke, we were heading up Cleggan bay. We tied up to the *Lenan Head* that was already beside the pier. The *Pride of Mace* came and tied up to us. The *Peggy G.* moored beside the *Regina Coeli*. There was a nimbus of gulls in the air.

CHAPTER TWENTY

I MENTIONED THE FORT of Grania—Grania, known also as Grania Uaile, in English, Grace O'Malley. She seems to have been a first-class sea pirate, having her headquarters on Clare Island, twelve miles to the north of Bofin. There, it is said, the cables of her galleys passed through a window of the castle, that of her fleetest ship-of-war being attached to her own bedpost. Her first husband, whom she had rescued from drowning before they were married, was killed in an ambuscade resulting from a local feud. Grania bided her time and, eventually, not only slew many of the clan that had committed the murder, but took possession of their castle, and made it one of her chief residences. Her second husband was Sir Richard Bourke, whom she married on condition that, at the end of a year, either could dissolve the partnership merely by saying to the other: 'I dismiss you.' During that year of matrimony Grania quietly filled all her husband's castles with her own followers so that when, at the end of the period, she gave him a curt dismissal, Sir Richard found that most of his property was in his wife's possession.

One story of this Amazon tells how being compelled through stress of weather to land at Howth she sought hospitality at the castle. The answer she received was that 'His lordship was at dinner and could not be disturbed.' Furious at such an insult she contrived to kidnap the eldest son of the house, and only restored him to his parents on the payment of a heavy ransom and the promise that whenever a Lord of Howth should sit at dinner his doors would remain open for the admission of all strangers. And so it was until 'our own little private war' of a few years ago. Since then the custom has not been revived.

I was told how Grania visited Queen Elizabeth, and how, when the queen held out her hand to her, Grania, who was a big woman, held out her hand, too, but just a little higher than the queen's so that Elizabeth had to raise her hand.

' "I'd like to make you a countess," said Elizabeth to her, after they'd been talking for a while.

' "Oh, but you can't do that," said Grania.

' "Why can't I?" said Elizabeth.

' "Amn't I a queen the same as yourself?" said Grania. 'And with that the two of them made great friends.

' "Isn't it a lovely day?" said Elizabeth.

' "A lovely day, thank God," says Grania.

' "And did ye have a nice journey?"

' "Fair enough," says Grania.

' "Would it be rough in the channel?" asks Elizabeth.

' "What's the channel?" asks Grania. "Have ye ever been in the Atlantic?"

' "It must be wild out there," says Elizabeth.

' "Wild isn't in it," says Grania.

'Even so, Elizabeth made her son the Earl of Mayo. The one that was after being born in a ship.'

Many legends have arisen about Grania, most of them

probably some distance from the truth. But legends often represent the ideals of the community from which they spring. So let us leave her at that. A fearless woman, revelling in 'alarums and excursions,' whom even the restraints of childbirth did not deter from man's activities.

CHAPTER TWENTY-ONE

ROBERT RUTTLEDGE joined us on Bofin. He came in search of 'Leach's fork-tailed petrels,' which had been suspected of nesting on these islands. Like their relatives the storm petrels, known to mariners as 'Mother Carey's chickens,' like also the shearwaters, these birds only come to shore in the nesting season. Because all three nest in burrows, or in crevices under stones, and because their movements on shore only take place during the hours of darkness, many conjectures as to their nesting habits have arisen in the past. Sailors will still tell you that the 'storms' never go ashore at all, but lay their single egg in the sea and then carry it under their wing, against their body, until it is hatched. They are right about the single egg, chalky white, but not about its incubation.

Except that the fork-tails call frequently when on the wing at night, and the storms are silent, both species have very similar habits at the nesting colony. But the fork-tail is a much rarer bird. Their only known breeding stations in Britain are on St. Kilda, the Flannans, and North Rona. There they excavate burrows for themselves about two inches in width and from two to four feet in length. At the end of that corridor, sometimes on the bare earth, sometimes in quite an elaborate nest of grass, roots, and stems, with perhaps sheep's wool and lichen added, they lay their egg. Both male and female birds take their turn at incubation, and though they are visited by their mate at night, and probably fed, they may remain on the nest for several days at a time.

Bofin did not produce nests of either the fork-tailed or storm petrel, but there was a possibility of finding them on Inishshark. On the day that we sailed a grey mist hung over everything. The sea was grey, the cliffs were grey, even tufts of pink thrift, clumps of London pride, and clusters of green samphire matched with the grey lichen on the rocks. It recalled Browning's line on a painting by Andrea del Sarto:

'A common greyness silvers everything.'

Landing on Shark we climbed to one of the highest points of the island, close to its western cliffs. Tremendous cliffs majestic in their forms; with kittiwakes nesting on the green ledges, and fulmars launching themselves from barest rock to soar and swoop and swoon and glide again. Far below, the sea insistent on the rocks, endlessly surging.

In the morning it had seemed as if the day might clear, but the afternoon left little doubt in our minds to the contrary. For an hour, and then another hour, we sat on the lee side of a turf stack. Because of its sloping sides it gave us little shelter. The doctor lit a fire with oddments of turf that lay about, but they were damp, and there was more smoke from them than heat. During brief intervals when the mist seemed to lighten we moved, seeking for signs of the petrels, but, though we found colonies of the storms, there was none of the fork-tails.

My job was, chiefly, to make drawings, and, once, as I

looked down into a yawning abyss, an islander came and
stood beside me. 'I was sitting out on that bench of rock
one day last year,' he said, pointing to a narrow ledge, a
few feet below the main level of the cliff, 'and I was watching the seals and the cormorants down below, when all of
a sudden I felt something twitching at my coat. I put my
hand back to see what it was, and, next moment, wasn't I
sitting up on the top of that hill behind us.'

No, he didn't know how it could happen. He had never
heard the like of it before.

The evening wore on, the light faded. An hour before
midnight I became separated from my companions. Acting
therefore on prearranged plans, I made my way downhill
across the boggy moorland to the track that led to the harbour. There was no one on the pier when I got there, but
there was a light in a cottage near by, and the door was
open.

'God save all here,' I said.

'And you, too,' came a chorus from within.

Seven men were inside and an elderly woman, the
'woman of the house.' Three of the men were sitting on a
bench, three sat on low chairs, one leant against a white-
washed ladder that led to the loft.

The old woman came forward from the fire and shook
hands with me. 'You're welcome,' she said.

One of the men put a chair for me before the fire. The
old woman put more turf on the fire and fanned the embers
with the lid of a saucepan. Then she sat back resting a
hand on each knee. She was so serene, so monumental.
She seemed as much a part of the house as the dresser and
its china that stood against the wall. I tried to imagine her
as a young woman coming to the house as a bride. I tried to
think of her as a young mother anxious for her child, still

more anxious, maybe, for her husband on the sea. But she did not seem ever to have been anything but the mother of grown-up children and the grandmother of children still in the cradle.

A son of the house came in. 'You're welcome,' he said, coming over and shaking hands with me. He took off his wet oilskin jacket and trousers. They had got no fish, he said.

The old woman filled the kettle and hung it over the fire. Then she sat back again, calm and placid. One of the men was speaking. 'I hear,' he said, 'that Teigue found the cross where he dreamt it. 'Tis above in the chapel now. 'Twas under the stones, where he seen it in his dream. Didn't he find it next day when he shifted the stones?'

The woman of the house was moving about. She seemed to be preparing tea for her son that had come in. 'Draw up now, and take some tea,' she said to me. And, when I turned, the table was laid.

They asked me if I had travelled far, and, when I told them about my visits to the tropics, and how I had made drawings under water, 'That's the kind of thing you'd read in a book and you wouldn't believe it,' they said. The idea of voluntarily going under the water seemed to them strange, but it pleased them very much that, were it not for the cold, I would have gone down outside their own harbour and drawn the seaweed there. The growth there is magnificent. The clustered columns of amber-coloured weed might be the pillars of some long-drowned church. As in a medieval pageant, pennons stream, banners wave, ribbons flutter; while the rosettes of crimson, emerald, and gold glint on a marbled floor.

It was long after midnight when we left the cottage, a night in which we could not distinguish sea from land.

Ruttledge and the doctor had found the same hospitality. Now, it was three of the men in that cottage who were to take us back to Bofin. We filed down the narrow lane to the pier. The mist was driving in from the sea, thicker than ever. We could just distinguish the black silhouette of the curragh being carried, bottom up, on the shoulders of two of the men. It was like some prehistoric monster going back to the sea. Bow first, they lifted it into the water. Then we clambered on board. Oars were already on their thole pins, and we headed into the night. Dark, jagged rocks rose up around us, and the spray of the waves breaking on them blew back into our faces. From six quick-beating oars six whirlpools of light shot by. Each following wave was crested with phosphorus, 'the eye of the sea.' We moved like a huge leaping fish, plunging and rising again, then skimming the surface. No word was spoken. On and on through the night, the sharp creak of the oars alternating with the gurgle of each swirling blade-pool. Blacker and blacker, the mist now turned to heavy rain. Then the water came smooth, and big, eddying globules of light slid astern from each blade. We were inside Bofin harbour though we could see no land. The curragh swung about and a receding wave left the stern aground. One by one we stepped ashore, timing our steps to each falling wave.

CHAPTER TWENTY-TWO

THE DOCTOR'S GOING as mad as them other fellows' was what they said when we proposed to spend a night on High Island. No one on Bofin or Shark would spend a night there, not for a hundred pounds. The island was haunted, every one knew that. They did their best to dissuade us. The weather did its best to that end also. Day after day the 'white packs' were in the sky, 'the moon was sick,' and the seal was in the harbour.

You can only land on High Island in the calmest weather. The wind must be from the north and there must be little of it. Except for one small creek on the south side of the island the cliffs rise vertically, two hundred feet. In that small creek there is a surge, even on the calmest day. You have to jump from the boat on to a steep face of rock, and waste no time in getting from that to higher ground.

But weather did suit us at last, and we reached the island in Michael's fishing-boat. Michael, Paddy, and the doctor were the first to attempt a landing. They succeeded, though the punt got thrown on a ledge of rock and was nearly swamped. Then Paddy came back for Ruttledge and myself. 'Come on now, Bob! Jump!' said Michael. 'That's the boy!' he added as I reached the rocks. But the seat of my trousers stayed behind on a nail.

So we were ashore with our provisions. Whether we would get off again next morning was another matter. A few years ago men from the mainland of Connemara had brought a woman with them to gather grass on the island while they were setting lobster-pots near to the cliffs. She managed to get ashore, but, by the time they came to take her off, the sea had risen, and they were compelled to leave her on the island, alone, until next day. All that night they kept fires going on the mainland, lest she should feel lonely, but she, 'with the dint of the fright that was on her,' gave birth that night to the child that she was carrying. 'But God is good. Wasn't everything that she wanted for herself and the child, food, clothes, and all, left down to her from heaven.'

Nick Dolan, the doctor, is typical of all good doctors in all good story-books. Untiring energy, never out of spirits, his only idea to minister to others who might for the time being have more specialized interests. 'Go on! To hell with the two of you! Put that kettle down. Say when you want tea and it will be ready. Leave everything where it is, and I'll find a place to camp. Get out of it, now.'

So Ruttledge went scouring the cliffs for petrels while I seized the last moments of daylight to make drawings among the ruins of the monastery that perches far out on this wind-swept plateau. No trees, no shrubs on the island, just a thick felt of grass starred with the pink flowers of bog pimpernel and centaury. There are no animals on

the island except rabbits and one goat, a large goat with
long horns that in the late evening rushed at us out of one
of the beehive cells. Of course it was only a goat. We were
quite sure of that, next morning.

The site of the monastery, built in the seventh century,
is on a narrow isthmus between two precipitous chasms.
At either side of the isthmus the remains of a cell balance
on the edge of the cliff. One of these cells is thought to
have been the scriptorium; a wild birthplace surely for
the missals and illuminated texts now so highly treasured.
Small wonder if, in such places as these, the scribe sometimes for a moment forgot his main purpose and added his
own more human thoughts.

Although I do not know of any interpolations that may
with certainty be attributed to the scribes of High Island,
many are to be found in other manuscripts of the period.
One poor man has written in the margin of his page: 'The
phlegm is upon me like a mighty river and my breathing
is laboured.' Another notes: 'Twenty nights from to-day
till Easter Monday, and I am cold and weary, without fire
or covering.' Another: 'Alas O hand, how much white
vellum hast thou written! Thou wilt make famous the vellum, while thou thyself wilt be the bare top of a faggot of
bones.' Some of the scribes were so carried away by the
story of their text that they could not refrain from com-
ment. After finishing the account of St. Peter's denial of
Christ one of them has written: 'By God, bad is the word
of his black oath, and bad is himself, and we do not say
which is the worse of them to-day.' Another, against the
mention of Judas Iscariot, has put the one word 'wretch.'
Other notes are in more cheerful vein. The man who at
the end of his text wrote 'Good-bye, little book' must have
been happy in his work. Likewise he who added: 'These

are things which I liked so much that I could not help copying them.'

For the most part the buildings on the island are in ruins, but one of the cells still retains its domed roof. There is a holy well, not far away, where Michael cured his toothache, and there are standing stones with incised crosses on many parts of the island. Everywhere about the ruins the ground is strewn with loose stones, and it was among these stones that we found our largest colony of storm petrels. We saw no sign of fork-tails on the island. From sunset on we had heard the storms underground, a long purring trill, ending with a quick, high-pitched 'chic,' or 'chicca'; 'pur-r-r-r-r-chicca, pur-r-r-r-r-chic.' An hour and a quarter after sunset we saw the first bird flying. Others followed, in quick succession. Soon the sky was full of them, darting here, flashing there. Quick as swallows, and silent as bats, they brushed past our heads. Out of the welter of stones they rose from all directions, in all directions. From under our feet, from far on the right, from near on the left, high up, low down, like dark arrows they shot past. For a moment the purring would cease, then a new note would be added, a rhythmic 'chick, chick, chick,' like the ticking of a clock.

These birds are saturated with oil; 'martin-oils,' they

call them in these parts, from their habit of sipping up floating oil from the surface of the sea. They can eject oil, too, from their mouths, and that right speedily, when handled; a noisome-smelling product to most noses. Their bodies are so impregnated with oil that, at one time, in some of the remote islands of the Hebrides, the inhabitants actually used them as candles. By passing a rush through the body it was found to burn as well as if dipped in tallow or any other grease.

The gable end of the monastery loomed darker and darker. One forgot the crying of the gulls, the hissing of the sea and its groan and gurgle in the caves below. 'Tic-tic, pur-r-r-r-r; tic-tic, pur-r-r-r-r, pur-r-r-r . . .' So it would last till dawn.

The doctor had collected dry turf from the roofs of shallow rabbit-burrows, and had built a fire. Now he came to tell us that the kettle was on the boil. Reluctantly we left the petrels and set out for the camp. Dark clouds overhead mingled with dark cliffs at our feet. It was only with difficulty that we could see the cliff edge. There was a sense of complete isolation in space, in infinite space, as far removed as a star from the rest of the world. If one of us spoke to another it was as if he called from far away. All sense of distance had gone.

Suddenly there fell upon us a deluge of sound, an almost smothering blanket of noise, a bedlam of screaming birds, hoarse and throaty. 'Cuc-cuc, coo-oo-oo; cuc-cuc, coo-oo-oo; kek-kek-curr-ur-ur; kik-kik-keu-eu.' Big black birds, they whizzed past our heads, all the time screaming. They sounded like barn-door cockerels with bronchitis; the last syllable was drawn back in a kind of nasal wheeze.

I thought of St. Patrick on the holy mountain, and how that 'after he had fasted many days the demons of paganism resolved to tempt and torment him. They therefore covered the whole mountain top in the form of vast flocks of hideous black birds, so dense that Patrick could see neither sky, nor earth, nor sea. They swooped down upon him and over him on their black wings, and with savage beaks they filled the air with discordant screams, making day and night horrible with their cries.'

But no one was tempting us that night. The birds were Manx shearwaters, who, like the petrels, came to their nests after dark.

Soon after the first gleam of dawn in the north-east the cries had died away. For another hour the purring of the petrels could be heard, then in the strengthening light there was silence save for the piccolo notes of a sea-pie or the whistle of a passing curlew. Then the wild vista of hills on the mainland came forth from its dew. And Michael came back with the sun.

CHAPTER TWENTY-THREE

HIGH ISLAND IS THOUGHT by many to have been the first
call of St. Brandon when in the sixth century he made
his great seven-year voyage into the western ocean. How
much of the story is true it is hard to say, probably not a
great deal. Yet it is a story which spread across Europe, the
geographers of Spain and Portugal describing the 'Island
of Sheep' and the 'Island of Birds' in words which must
surely have been taken from the Christian legend. Going
further east, we find, in the tale of *Sinbad the Sailor,* several
points of similarity and one identical incident. It seems
highly probable that the saint did set out in a vessel of
'wicker sides, covered with cow-hide' akin to the curraghs
of laths and tarred canvas that are in use to-day all along
the western and south-western coast of Ireland. It would
seem, too, that he visited many islands which still exist and
possibly others which no longer exist, that he was, in fact, a
Christian Ulysses. But if he ever wrote his story it has been
lost, and that version which now tells of his travels, with
many embellishments, dates from five centuries later.

St. Brandon set out from Kerry with fourteen of his
monks to find the Island of the Blest, 'to-fore the gates of
Paradyse, where as is ever daye, and never night. . . . But
or they entred into the shyppe they fasted XL dayes, and

lyved devoutly, and eche of them receyved the sacrament.
. . . And then saynt Brandon badde the shypmen to
wynde up the sayle, and forth they sayled in Goddes name,
so that on the morow they were out of syght of ony londe;
and XL dayes and XL nightes after they sayled playn eest,
and than they sawe an ylonde ferre fro them, and they
sayled thyderwarde as fast as they coude, and they sawe a
grete roche of stone appere above all the water, and thre
dayes they sayled aboute it or they coude gete in to the
place. But at the last, by the purveyaunce of God, they
founde a lytell haven, and there went a-londe everychone.'

After being entertained on the island, presumably in
that monastery in which the petrels now make their nests,
'they returned agayne to theyr shyppe and sayled a longe
tyme in the see after or they coude fynde ony londe, tyll at
the last, by the purveyaunce of God, they sawe ferre fro
them a full fayre ylonde, ful of grene pasture, wherein were
the whytest and gretest shepe that ever they sawe; for every
shepe was as grete as an oxe.'

Then they sailed again, and this time we get one of
several parallels to incidents in the *True History* of Lucian,
for the saint and his followers landed on an island that
turned out to be a mighty sea monster. Having left their
fire and meat behind them and 'mervayled sore' they took
to their ship and sailed west three days and three nights
without seeing land. 'But soone after, as God wold, they
sawe a fayre ylonde, full of floures, herbes, and trees,
wherof they thanked God of his good grace, and anone they
went on londe. And whan they had gone longe in this, they
founde a ful fayre well, and thereby stode a fayre tree, full
of bowes, and on every bough sate a fayre byrde, and they
sate so thycke on the tree that unneth ony lefe of the tree
myght be seen, the nombre of them was so grete, and they

songe so meryly that it was an hevenly noyse to here.
Wherefore saynt Brandon kneled down on his knees, and
wepte for joye, and made his prayers devoutely unto our
Lord God to knowe what these byrdes ment. And than
anone one of the byrdes fledde fro the tree to saynt Brandon, and he with flykerynge of his wynges made a full mery
noyse lyke a fydle, that hym semed he herde never so joyfull a melodye. And than saynt Brandon commaunded the
byrde to tell hym the cause why they sate so thycke on the
tree, and sange so meryly. And than the byrde sayd, "Som-
tyme we were aungels in heven, but whan our mayster
Lucyfer fell down into hell for his hygh pryde, we fell with
hym for our offences, some hygher, and some lower, after
the qualyté of theyr trespace, and bycause our trespace is
but lytell, therfore our Lorde hath set us here out of all
payne in full grete joye and myrth, after his pleasynge, here
to serve hym on this tree in the best maner that we can."
. . . And than all the byrdes began to synge evensonge so
meryly, that it was an hevenly noyse to here.'

After eight weeks on the island the voyagers set out
again. They revisited the Island of Shepe, met again 'the
grete fysshe,' and, buffeted by tempests, landed on many
islands, even seeing hell, with Judas in everlasting torment,
until they came to the 'fayrest countree eestwarde that ony
man myght se.' It was 'so clere and bryght that it was an
hevenly syght to beholde.' Here they tarried forty days and
it was always day and never night. 'And at the last they
came to a ryver, but they durst not go over. And there
came to them a fayre yonge man, and welcomed them
curtoysly, and called eche of them by his name, and dyd
grete reverence to saynt Brandon, and sayd to them, 'Be ye
now joyfull, for this is the londe that ye have sought; but
our Lorde wyll that ye departe hens hastely, and he wyll

shewe to you more of his secretes whan ye come agayn into
the see; and our Lorde wyll that ye lade your shyppe with
the fruyte of this londe, and hye you hens, for ye may no
longer abyde here, but thou shalt sayle agayne into thyne
owne countree, and soone after thou comest home thou
shalt dye.'

So, after glimpsing paradise, 'they toke their leve and
went to shyppe . . . and came home into Yrelonde in
safeté.'

Five of these early 'Imrama,' or sea tales, have come
down to us, of which the most important are the voyages of
Bran, of Maelduin, and of St. Brandon. The first two are,
for the most part, pagan in spirit, with descriptions of a
paradise not unlike what Christians are led to believe is
expected by followers of Mohammed. But the third is entirely and devoutly Christian, though many of the earlier
themes appear again in different form.

Many of the islands referred to in the story may well
have been more than legendary. The tales of lost islands,
Atlantis, Antilla, Hy Brazil, and many others off the western coast of Europe, are numerous. As late as the end of
the sixteenth century the Spaniards and Portuguese believed in the existence of St. Brandon's Isle. Until 1865 Hy
Brazil was marked on the charts. Columbus and his crew
most certainly believed in the existence of large islands in
mid ocean. Brazil and the Antilles, in the New World,
acquired their names through mistaken geography.

Geologists tell us that there have been changes in the
sea-floor of the Atlantic. Botanists say that the existence on
the west coast of Ireland of such plants as the luxuriant
Mediterranean heath, the large-belled St. Dabeoc's heath,
and, curiously enough, that saxifrage known as London
pride, which appear nowhere else in the British Isles but

are characteristic of the Spanish peninsula and the south-west of France, points to the fact that, at one time, there was a continuous coastline from Ireland to Spain. Zoologists corroborate by producing a slug, a snail, a beetle, and a woodlouse from Ireland which, unknown in Great Britain, occur in south-western Europe.

But undoubtedly the mirages which are still seen from the mainland and from the Aran Isles have much to do with perpetuating the belief in these spectral islands. From educated and uneducated alike we get almost identical stories of islands that have appeared to them far out to sea, islands with trees and houses, and, in some cases, even cattle and sheep browsing on the slopes. Mr. Thomas J. Westropp, M.A., M.R.I.A., has seen Hy Brazil three times and even made a coloured sketch of it. Describing the last experience he wrote: 'It was a clear evening, with a fine golden sunset, when, just as the sun went down, a dark island suddenly appeared far out to sea, but not on the horizon. It had two hills, one wooded; between these, from a low plain, rose towers and curls of smoke.' His mother, his brother, and several friends also saw it at the same time.

It is believed in County Clare that if the man who sees the phantom can throw a handful of earth at it, without taking his eyes off the vision, the enchantment will be broken, and the island restored to its place among the Arans. But no one has yet managed to pick up the soil without, momentarily, glancing downward, and so the spell remains.

CHAPTER TWENTY~FOUR

My visit to the Arans was in search of something more solid than spectral islands. I wanted to see Dun Aenghus, the Fort of Aenghus, 'the most magnificent barbaric monument in Europe.' I wanted to see the other forts: Dun Oghil, the Fort of the Oak Wood; Dun Cathair, the Black Fort; Dun Eoghanacta, called after the descendants of Eoghan Mor, who owned the southern half of Ireland in the second century; all of them on Inishmore, the most northerly of the three islands. There was also Dun Conor on Inishmaan, the middle island, while on all three islands there were numerous churches from the earliest days of Christianity, days when the islands were known as Ara of the Saints, a centre of religion and culture to which men flocked, even from Rome.

Dun Aenghus *is* superb. It stands out there on that high cliff, three hundred feet above the sea, proud, almost arrogant against the ceaseless battling of sea and sky. Splendid masonry. No speck of mortar. Mighty stones one on another, 'well and truly laid.' To-day its three walls are crescentic. Whether they were ever circular, no one can say. Even in our own time part of the cliff has eroded, and with it many stones of the walls have fallen. But what need was there for defences along the edge of a precipice that no mortal could ever hope to climb? At most a shallow barrier would suffice, lest in the daylight a child should lose its balance, lest in black night a man should step too far.

The inner wall of the citadel, to-day, stands twelve feet high. At its base its combined terraces measure eighteen feet from face to face. A second wall, still mighty, though but half that thickness, follows irregularly the line of the first. A third, in a wider sweep, encloses eleven acres. But outside the second wall there is a feature inhibiting in appearance and almost impossible of negotiation. For a varying depth of from ten to twenty-five yards tall standing stones, weather-worn to razor-like edges, stand, thickly set, in the way of all intruders. To pass through such a barrier under a hail of arrows or other missiles would, indeed, have been an ordeal.

Equally impressive is Dun Cathair, though there is but the one wall here, cutting almost straight across the narrowest point of a bleak headland. That wall, again, is eighteen feet in thickness and almost as high. Outside it there is an abattis twice as wide as at Dun Aenghus. At Dun Eoghanacta, as at Dun Oghil and again at Dun Conor, the defences are circular, and almost as powerful.

Of the history of these great forts there is little known with certainty. Even in the year 1014 it was but a legend. Professor R. A. S. Macalister, in his book *Ireland in Pre-Celtic Times*, writes: 'I know nothing in any country more stimulating to the imagination than the problem which these extraordinary fortresses present to the archaeologist. Huge structures stand on those barren islands, and we ransack tradition and history in vain for the smallest ray of light as to their origin.'

One day as I walked back from Dun Oghil I met an old man carrying a scythe. He was dressed in the usual speckled blue homespun of the island and wore the rawhide pampooties on his feet.

'Tell me,' he said, 'are ye any good at riddles?'

'I might be,' I said.

'Go down on your knees,' he said.

I did so.

Resting his scythe against the wall and picking up handfuls of small stones he got down on the road beside me. There, slowly and with great care, he arranged eleven of the stones into the form of a cross, seven of them for the upright and two at either side on a level with the fifth. 'Now,' he said, counting them, 'there's one, two, three, four, five, six, seven if you go straight up, and there's one, two, three, four, five, six, seven if you go up and turn to the right, and there's one, two, three, four, five, six, seven if ye go up and turn to the left. Isn't that right?'

'It is,' I said.

'Now,' he said, 'I'll take two away, one from eyther side of the cross, d'ye see, and I'll move the two that are left up one, and now there's seven still left whichever way ye count. Isn't that so?'

'It is,' I said.

'And isn't it wonderful?'

'It is, indeed.'

'Did ye ever see the like of that riddle?'

'Never!'

'Then I'll show ye another one.'

This time he collected twenty-one stones, one of them bigger than the others, and arranged them in a circle on the road. 'That big one is an Irishman, and 'tis the way they are all on board of a ship and they has nothin' to ate. And they's going to ate each other. But the Irishman's wife is the cook and she doesn't want to cook her husband at all. I suppose 'twas fond of him she was. " 'Tis I'll do the counting," says she. So she stands all the men round her in a circle like them stones. "Now," says she, " 'tis eleven days we are without a bite of food," so she counts off eleven of the men from her husband. 'Keep your eye on that stone, now,' said he, pointing to the eleventh stone from the big one. "Now," says she, "there's seven days in a week, so we'll count seven and we'll ate the seventh man, and then we'll count seven again and we'll ate the seventh man again, and so we'll go on till there's none of us left." ' So starting with number twelve in the ring the old man began counting, and every seventh stone that he reached he threw it out of the circle. When there were less than seven left he con-

tinued the count a second time round until, when there
were but two remaining, the count began and ended with
the smaller of the stones. 'And there's the Irishman left,'
said he, with great pride.

He rose from his knees on the dusty road, and I was glad
to do the same.

'Did you ever see the like of that?' he asked.

'Never,' I said.

'Isn't that the grandest riddle in the world?'

'It is, indeed.'

'There never was a better,' he said. Then he took up his
scythe. 'I must be getting along to cut rye in the west. Good
day to you now.'

'Good day to you,' I said, and with that we parted.

Now, truth to tell, there are many similar 'riddles,' and
many versions of each of them.

Mr. Gerard Murphy, in the *Journal of the Folk-lore of
Ireland Society,* 1942, tells how one of them has its variants
in medieval Latin, among the Arabs of the fourteenth century, among the Japanese and Scandinavians in the seventeenth and eighteenth centuries, among the Indians in
modern times, and among English-, French-, Italian-, and
German-speaking peoples from the sixteenth century on-
wards.

That particular problem, 'The Puzzle of the Thirty
Counters,' is concerned with arranging fifteen black and
fifteen white counters in a circle in such a way that by
counting round that circle and throwing out every ninth
counter the blacks will become separated from the whites.
In most versions the dilemma occurs on board a ship, and
concerns the choice of those who must be thrown over-
board to lighten the load. In Christian versions of the story
it is usually Jews or Mohammedans who are found super-

fluous, while in Jewish or Mohammedan versions the compliment is, very naturally, reversed. In Japan the struggle is between children and stepchildren; in India it is between honest men and thieves. In Ireland one version, at least, concerns a fight, a more or less domestic little affair after a bit of matchmaking. All had gone well, the marriage had been arranged, the two sides were happy, and everybody had drunk and sung and danced far into the night. But, just before they went to bed, one of the men by name of Aodh stood up to the fire to warm the backs of his legs, and another by the name of Conan, who was already lying down by the fire, couldn't resist the temptation of hitting him behind the knees with the back of his sword. The result was that Aodh was 'left sitting on his buttocks in the fire.' Needless to say, he leapt out of it pretty quick and he went for Conan, and I don't blame him either, and somebody else went for Aodh, and before you could wink one eye there were no two in the house that weren't at each other's throats. Then the bride-to-be stood up. 'Men,' said she, 'this is more like a murder house than a wedding house, but I'll settle it all for ye if ye'll give me five minutes of time.'

And so she arranged them, and so she counted them that she kept all her own people on one side of the door, and all her husband's people on the other side of the door, and so she quietened them, and afterwards they all came together again, and they drank and they sang and they danced and they had a grand night until the morning.

For the benefit of my readers who may find themselves in a similar difficulty on sea or land I append the magic words that solve the problem:

'From numbers' aid and art
Never will fame depart.'

All that is necessary is to pick out the vowels as they appear in the couplet, thus: O U E A I A A E E I A E E A, and give to the A, E, I, O, U the respective values 1, 2, 3, 4, 5. In this way we get 4 5 2 1 3 1 1 2 2 3 1 2 2 1, and taking B for black and W for white, and using them alternately, the solution appears:

B B B B W W W W W B B W B B B W B W W B B W W W B W W B B W

Arrange your party in that order, count out every ninth man or woman, and there'll be no more trouble.

CHAPTER TWENTY~FIVE

THERE ARE MANY ancient churches on the Arans and they stand on the most varied sites. Among them, the oratory of St. Benen is high on a bare hill, St. Gobnet's is tucked away under a cliff, that of St. Cavan is on the shore, almost buried in sand, while Kilcananagh is one of those hard naked limestone terraces so typical of the islands. All four are minute in size though their masonry is cyclopean. The external measurements of Teampull Benen are fifteen feet by eleven; internally it is little more than ten by seven. This church differs from the others in that its axis runs north and south so that its one window, to the east, is in a side wall. From there the kneeling saint would have looked across a valley where, in years to come, a monastery with its round tower would dominate the scene. Only the base of the tower now remains, a dozen of its eighty feet. These round towers, as Petrie has demonstrated, were not of pagan origin, but were built to serve the dual purpose of belfry and fortress for the adjoining monastery. Contrary to earlier theories, which suggested that the towers had been built by the Danes, were of Phoenician genesis, or had been used for phallic worship, Petrie has shown that they are never found unconnected with ancient ecclesiastical foundations, that their style of architecture exhibits no features not found in the churches with which they are connected, and that they possess, invariably, features not found in Ireland in pagan times. In height they vary from fifty to a hundred and fifty feet, their circumference at the base being from forty to sixty feet: tall, tapering columns capped by a conical roof of stone. They have few windows, and then but small and at a considerable height. Their entrance, low and narrow, may be from eight to thirty feet above the ground, and often shows evidence of having been provided with double doors. There can be no doubt that they were regarded, and often used, as keeps, not only for the valuables of the monasteries, but for the ecclesiastics themselves during the raids that in those times were by no means infrequent. In the *Annals of the Four Masters*, that compilation of ancient Irish history made in the Abbey of Donegal during the years 1632-6, we read: 'A.D. 948. The belfry of Slane burned by the foreigners, with its full of relics and distinguished persons, together with Caineachair, Lector of Slane, and the crosier of the patron saint, and a bell, the best of bells.' In the *Annals of Ulster* we read that in the year 1013 the great stone church of Armagh was burned by the Danes, together with the belfry and its bells. In the *Annals of Inisfallen* it is recorded that in 1127 a number of persons took refuge in the belfry of Trim when Conor MacFergall O'Lochlinn came hosting from Donegal, but that it availed them little for the tower was set on fire and they all lost their lives.

Near to the tower, on Aran, is the shaft of a high cross, richly decorated with strange animals, intricate plait-work, and interlacing spirals. I often think how akin to Irish manner and temperament these carvings are. Wild imaginings, richness of phrasing, unexpected changes of subject, inconsequent turns of humour. 'Yes,' said a man to me, in one sentence, 'we got a dozen and a half fine trout and the Russians have got Kharkov, I know well enough the bitch has got worms, but look at that poor fellow Paddy, drunk again, and the thoughts his mother had for him when he was born!' And how like the music of the jigs and reels, too, are those interlacings and spirals with their continuous yet ever varied and always exciting repetition of the same theme.

The high crosses of Ireland, of which more than fifty still exist, are, like the round towers, a subject in themselves, and much has been written about them. Dating from the tenth to the thirteenth century, they are among the most impressive memorials of the countryside, not so much for their size—few exceed fifteen feet in height—as for their wealth of sculptural detail and significance. In some of the earlier of these monuments the abstract plait-work and spirals already mentioned are predominant, but in the later crosses the designs become completely representational. Not only were the front and back richly carved, but the sides of the shaft, the upper and lower surfaces of the arms, and even the ends of the arms held their quota of symbolism. This symbolism eventually became organized into

a definite iconographic scheme, a succession of subjects
from Old and New Testaments. It is true that some of the
crosses were monumental or commemorative, but their
chief purpose seems to have been to bring more clearly before unlettered minds the main events of Bible history. All
the crosses have the typical Celtic circle or wheel, and it
would seem that the effect of many of the carvings was, originally, heightened by the addition of colour.

St. Gobnet, whose name is sometimes anglicized to St.
Judith, lived in the sixth century.

'You haven't met St. Gobnet? Oh, but you must meet
her! She's lovely! You'd love her! She blinds your enemies
for you. Sure, every time the inspector comes into the office
I whisper to St. Gobnet, and he never sees a wrong entry.'

That was said to me in County Cork, where, as also in
County Limerick, the saint is highly venerated. It is told
of her how once, when the countryside was being invaded
by a neighbouring chieftain, she went out to meet the ad-
vancing host, carrying with her a small hive of bees. When
she saw the approaching enemy she prayed, and forthwith
the bees issued from their hive and attacked the eyes of the
invaders. So were they driven back and their ravages stayed.

Natives of County Cork will claim that that happened in
the valley of the Lee, but in County Limerick, in the townland of Kilgobinet, people will show you a hillock on the
Fair-Green whereon St. Gobnet stood to blind the enemy.
In proof of that they will tell you that any young man who,
having prayed at the Holy Well, close by, stands on that
hillock on St. Gobnet's day, the 11th of February, and in-
vokes the saint will certainly make a good match within the
coming year. Whether in this there is any subtle connection
with temporary blindness I did not find out.

I was told no legend of the bees on Aran, but a thorn-tree

a few yards from St. Gobnet's oratory was pointed out to me. The speaker said that once he had transplanted that tree nearer to the church, but that next morning it was back in the spot from which he had taken it.

On the islands there are many holy wells. In one of them on Inisheer there is water that will only boil when all the other wells on the island have gone dry.

There are also many standing crosses, among them one on Inishmore, a slab with incised pattern. Above the cross there is a circle, symbol of eternity, and above the circle there is a hole, pierced through from side to side. Cloths passed through that hole became more efficacious as bandages; handkerchiefs passed through will find lovers for young maids.

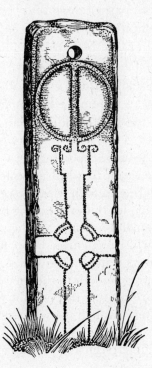

I went to Inisheer by curragh from the north island, calling at Inishmaan, middle island, on the way. Three brothers manned the oars. Two government inspectors, one for employment, the other for unemployment, sat in the stern. I was in the bow. The oars in the west of Ireland, both on lake and sea, pivot on a single thole-pin. Such niceties as 'feathering' are unknown. At any moment one's hands may be needed. In the curraghs there are no seats for passengers. They sit on the bottom. Nothing but a few laths and a strip of tarred canvas between you and many fathoms.

In perfect time the six narrow-bladed oars splashed in the water. All in time they creaked on their pins. Swosh, swarsh, swuurrsh, swash, under my stern in the bow of the boat. Three huge backs before me, three wild, wind-blown forelocks over three pair of deep-set eyes constantly glancing behind their shoulders. Heavy tweeds, heavy flannels, muscles heaving their double strokes. Thole-pins creaking. Swash, swash, swurrsh, under my stern.

On the return journey there was a following wind. As in an arm-chair, I sat in the bow with an arm on either gunwale. We did not stop at the middle island.

> A sail is set but the oars keep swinging,
> Fast as the breeze we move, white crests following,
> Roaring through the sea with white waves after,
> White waves racing us, but ever falling back.
> Passing Inishmaan and its silver beaches
> Whimbrels rise whistling, curlews, too, fly calling;
> Sea-pies and plovers watchful as we pass,
> And the sea running smooth in the shelter of the land.
> Fast as a fish we are rushing through the water,
> Through the water, through the water, and the sail is full,
> Golden blades are swinging, scarce splashing as they cleave,
> And white foam, in crescents, breaks all along the hull.

CHAPTER TWENTY~SIX

Back in Galway everybody was talking about the event of the year, THE RACES. Six months earlier I had been asked if I was staying for THE RACES. 'Everybody goes mad for THE RACES,' I was told. And now everybody was preparing to go mad. Crowds were arriving daily in the city, from Dublin, from Limerick, from Cork, and from everywhere else in Ireland. A fair, with all its tents and wagons, its hurdy-gurdies, merry-go-rounds, swings, and other amusements, had established itself in the Square. No one thought of going to bed before four o'clock in the morning. If he had thought of it it wouldn't have been much help to him.

A momentary cloud had hung over the preliminaries when someone in authority had hinted that the new laws required the licensed houses to close for a few hours each night. Such a thing had never been heard of during Galway race week. But when it was realized that there were far more licensed houses in the town than police the cloud vanished. The houses just stayed open.

Every room in every hotel in the city had been booked, months ahead. Every room in every hotel within a day's journey of the racecourse had been booked for months ahead. Now that I saw the crowds and heard the 'loud-speaking' dance bands blaring into the early hours of each morning I began to regret my earlier enthusiasm. Every hour produced a new fanfare. Cacophony competed with cacophony.

Two days before the event a man came up to me in the street. 'You're from Cork, I'd know you anywhere,' he said. 'When are you coming back? They're all asking for you. There's Lizzie and Henry Hennessy at Carrigrohane, and Dan Buckley at the post office there, and Jerry Linehan that posed for you awhile, he says he was your first "noodist" model, and I was talking to George Logan at Ballinora, who has your father's watch—you used to poach his bogs— and there's fellows that was with you in the Munsters; they're all asking for you.'

'Don't say another word,' I said. 'I'm going back to-morrow.'

So next morning—to hell with the races—I stood in front of the station booking-office before it was open, and, as I stood, I remembered another Irishman who had once stood at the booking-office at Euston station. 'Give me a ticket,' he said, when his turn in the queue brought him opposite the window.

'Where to?' asked the booking-clerk, somewhat haughtily.

'To Cork, of course. Where the divil else?'

And to Cork I was going, too. Where the divil else!

Cork is the loveliest city in the world. Anybody who doesn't agree with me either was not born there or is prejudiced. The streets are wide, the quays are clean, the bridges are noble. Two wide channels of the river reflect the glittering limestone buildings. To quote Spenser:

> 'The spreading Lee, that like an island fayre,
> Encloseth Cork with his divided flood.'

It is such a friendly city, too. People that you have never met in your life stop you in the street to say that they knew a relation of yours. A complete stranger put his card into my hand. 'Will you dine with me at the club to-night?' he said. It often seemed that the quickest way to get from one end of Patrick Street to the other, a matter of six hundred yards, would be to take a taxi and tell the driver to make a detour of twenty miles. First it is a man outside a pub who says to you: 'Wisha, captain, how are you? Sure, I'm Clancy your batman. And have you still got the belt? 'Twas the loveliest belt in the battalion.' And then, outside a book-shop, it's a dean or an archdeacon that you first knew as a curate. 'I remember your father,' said one of them, 'saying to me: "There's that poor boy of mine upstairs wasting his time trying to be an artist." ' And then it's an old lady who says: 'I hope you still go to church, Bob? Your father often used to tell me how you would button up his cassock for him.' And then it would be a girl with hair like a furnace and eyes calm pools of blue, and she would say: 'Do you re-member me?' And I'd say 'Of course I do, you're Madge,' and she would say: 'Indeed, I'm not, I'm Peg'; and then we'd go and have tea together and she would want to know all about Madge.

Even to get a call through on the telephone may entail a conversation. 'Hold on a while now and I'll see if I can get him for you. I have an idea he was away shooting for the week-end, but I'll see if I can get him. Isn't it a grand day? Yerra, 'tis like summer. Another fortnight now and we'll be into spring. Tell me, who am I speaking to? Oh, to be sure, I know you well. I saw you the other night. "Who's that?" said I to Paddy Riordan. You remember Paddy, he lived at the cross below you. "Sure, that's Bob Gibbings," says he, "the fellow is writing a book about Cork." Hold

on a while, I think you're through. Ah, you're not. I'm
Mick Ahern that lived at Curraheen. You wouldn't re-
member me, but—hold on a while—'tis wonderful weather.
Did you see any widgeon when you were down at Imokilly?
They tell me the place is full of them. Oh, indeed, yes, I
saw you getting on to the bus. 'Tis a grand spot down there.
Hold on a while, you're through. Good-bye now and good
luck, you're through.'

Of the architecture, Macaulay said of University College, that 'it is worthy to stand in the High Street of
Oxford.' The Father Matthew Memorial Church has as
delicate a spire as one could find in the four kingdoms. The
campanile of Shandon would be an ornament in any town
in Italy. Lest there should be man or woman alive so igno-
rant as not to have heard of that poem *The Bells of Shandon,* written by Father Francis Mahony, I print the first
verse. The remainder may be read in the *Oxford Book of
English Verse.*

'With deep affection
And recollection
 I often think of
    Those Shandon bells,
Whose sounds so wild would,
In the days of childhood,
Fling round my cradle
    Their magic spells.
On this I ponder
Where'er I wander,
And thus grow fonder,
    Sweet Cork, of thee;
With thy bells of Shandon
That sound so grand on
The pleasant waters
    Of the River Lee.'

The author, while a student in Rome, wrote the lines during a fit of home-sickness, and pinned them over his bed. Later in life, after some years of clerical duties in Ireland, he went to London and Paris and became a 'Bohemian.' He was a brilliant linguist and amused himself by translating the works of poets, from Chaucer to Tom Moore, into Greek, Latin, French, and Italian. These he published in a series of witty essays, *The Reliques of Father Prout,* which, with transparent solemnity, purported to show that the source of the poets' writings was plagiarism rather than inspiration. Of course, nobody believed him. Neither did he wish that they should.

It would be easy to compile a list of famous men, saints, prelates, scientists, artists, statesmen, who were born in the city and county of Cork. But that would be commonplace. Any town can do as much, though perhaps not so much. It would be easy, too, to compile a list of Cork women who in the more orthodox walks of life have achieved distinction, especially in literature. But I would rather tell of three who, by less conventional roads, reached fame. There was the Hon. Elizabeth Aldworth, the only woman ever to become a freemason. There was Miss Thompson who became Empress of Morocco. There was Anne Bonny, who became a pirate.

It was at one time thought that Mrs. Aldworth, who at that time was Miss St. Leger, had hidden herself, deliberately, in a clock in order to spy on the masonic ceremonies being held in Doneraile Court, her father's house. But that legend may now be dismissed, having no other authority than the words of a poem published a hundred and twenty-seven years later. From evidence more recently collected it would seem that the lady, then not more than nineteen years of age, had fallen asleep in the library of her home, a room adjoining that in which the 'lodge' was being held. Structural alterations between the two rooms had been in progress and were not yet complete. Miss St. Leger woke up to see light shining through unfilled crevices in the temporary wall, and, prompted by a not unnatural curiosity, she removed one or two of the bricks, thereby being enabled to watch the proceedings. Suddenly realizing the seriousness of her actions she tried to escape, but it was then too late. After a lengthy discussion among the members it was decided that there was only one course open, and we read that the 'fair culprit, with a high sense of honour, at once consented to pass through the impressive ceremonials she had already in part witnessed.'

Of Miss Thompson I quote from Broughton's *A Six Years' Residence in Algiers*. Under the date 21st January 1818 he writes:

'Mr. Clarke told me the following curious story: That

when he was at Alicant a galley arrived, which had just escaped from Tangiers with the first or favourite wife of Muli Mahomed, the late Emperor of Morocco, who had lately been assassinated by his rebellious son Muli Ishmael. This lady, who, with her attendants, was seeking a refuge in Spain, was originally a Miss Thompson of Cork, and when on her passage from that city to Cadiz on a matrimonial expedition, she had been captured by a Moorish corsair, and made a slave. Her first intended bridegroom had been a Mr. Shee, an Irish merchant settled at Cadiz, who, during a visit he had made to his native country, had become acquainted with and attached to Miss Thompson, who possessed great charms. . . . The lady, in fulfilment of her promise, sailed to join her future husband; but as just narrated her destiny was changed by the capture of the vessel she was in by a Marroquin corsair, which carried her into Fez. Here Miss Thompson was detained as a slave, and closely confined, until a report of her uncommon beauty having reached the Emperor, Muli Mahomed, she was by his orders removed to the imperial palace, and every inducement was held out to her to embrace the Mahomedan faith, and to accede to the Emperor's desire of making her his wife. Whether it was by persuasion or from the conviction that her fate was irrevocably decided, her various scruples were overcome, and she became the wife of Muli Mahomed, and subsequently the mother of two sons, who bore the names, the eldest of Muli Ishmael, and the younger of Muli Mahomed. She was ever the most favoured of her imperial husband's wives, for he had many besides; and the number must have been great, as I have heard both from Mr. Clark and Mr. Romans, who was at one time established as a merchant in Morocco, that the Emperor, Muli Mahomed, actually formed a regiment, composed entirely of his own sons, to the number of five hundred and twenty-three, most of them being blacks.'

Anne Bonny was born in Kinsale, a seaport town in which I spent seven years of my own youth. It is a historic town, once the most important port in Ireland, with ancient forts on either side of its harbour, one named after James II, who landed there, and the other after Charles II. It received its first charter from Edward III, A.D. 1334. Its corporation mace with detachable head, for use as a loving cup, is now the property of the mayor and aldermen of Margate, the government of Kinsale being at present vested in town councillors.

It is a town which breeds strong characters. I knew a man there who couldn't do less than forty miles as an afternoon spin on his bicycle, and that at full speed up hill and down hill over roads that in those days were far from perfect. His 'call,' when he stopped for refreshments, was a dozen of stout. He was a big man and he had a big family. He bought everything for them himself. If a daughter wanted a dress length he bought a bale of the material and served it out all round. If a reel of thread was wanted he bought a gross. One day he offered to clean my bicycle. He took it to pieces completely, removing every nut and screw, even taking out the bearings and washing them separately in paraffin. There were no half measures with him. I have seen his wife stemming strawberries into a wash-hand-basin, so that he might have his fruit after dinner.

Anne Bonny, though the daughter of a lawyer, was born outside the law. From the first she was 'of a fierce and courageous temper,' and from what we read of her early years there seems to have been little in her upbringing that would have tended to mellow these qualities. After journeying with her father to Carolina, and thence, with a poor specimen of a husband, to the island of Providence in the West Indies, she 'became acquainted with *Rackam* the Pyrate, who making Courtſhip to her, ſoon found Means of withdrawing her Affections from her Husband, ſo that ſhe conſented to elope from him, and go to Sea in Men's Cloaths.'

It is related that in their subsequent expeditions, 'when any business was to be done in their way, no body was more forward or courageous than she.' Eventually they were taken and sentenced to be hanged, but she, because of her condition at the time, was reprieved. On the day of Rackam's execution she was allowed to visit him, but all the consolation that she could offer was that 'if he had fought like a man he need not have been hanged like a dog.'

So much for the versatility of Cork women.

But even to live near County Cork is an asset. There was the 'Old Countess of Desmond,' whose home was only across the River Blackwater. All the soft westerly and south-westerly airs that she breathed had blown to her over County Cork. She lived to the age of at least a hundred and forty, some say a hundred and sixty-two, and only died then after falling out of a tree into which she had climbed to gather fruit. Earliest mention of the 'Old Countess' is found in Sir Walter Raleigh's *History of the World,* wherein he mentions her as being known to him, person-ally, while he was resident on his estates in County Cork. He speaks of her as 'having been married in the reign of King Edward IV' and as 'being alive in 1589,' and 'many years afterwards, as all the noblemen and gentlemen in Munster can witness.' Edward IV died in 1483, so even if the countess was married at the age of fifteen that would make her age in 1589 to be one hundred and twenty-one, and Raleigh says that she lived for many years after that.

The earliest date given for her death is 1604, making her minimum age one hundred and thirty-six years, but the more general computation adds another few years to that total.

Francis Bacon mentions her in his *History of Life and Death* as an instance of the longevity of the Irish, and when, in his *Natural History,* he is discussing teeth, he writes: 'They tell a tale of the old Countess of Desmond, who lived until she was seven score years old, that she did dentize twice or thrice, casting her old teeth, and others coming in their place.' Of her death it was written: 'She might have lived much longer had she not mett with a kind of violent death, for shee must needs climb a nutt tree, to gather nutts; soe falling down, she hurt her thigh, which brought on fever, and that brought death.'

CHAPTER TWENTY~SEVEN

THE NAME CORK is derived from the Irish *corcaig*, a marsh, for at one time the site of the present city was scarcely more than a swamp. There is a suggestion that the oldest part of the city was built by the Danes. If it was, those same Danes did their best in later years to nullify their earlier efforts, for in the years 820, 833, 837, 913, 960, and many others, they ravaged and ransacked the city.

Coming to more recent history we find that, in the year 1493, Perkin Warbeck appeared in the city in the character of Richard Plantagenet, Duke of York. He was received and entertained by the mayor with all princely honours, for which offence the king deprived the city of its charter and the mayor of his head.

In 1589 Sir Francis Drake with five ships of war, being chased by the Spaniards, sailed into Cork harbour and anchored in what has since been known as Drake's Pool in the Carrigaline river. It is a high wooded valley well screened from the outer harbour, and the Spaniards not seeing the entrance sailed away discomfited.

On 9th August 1617 Sir Walter Raleigh sailed from Cork harbour on his last unfortunate expedition to the West Indies. It has been said that 'the little we know of Raleigh in Ireland is not to his credit, excepting only his introduc-

tion of the potatoe.' But it is doubtful if he even did so
much. William Bowles, born near Cork about 1705, in his
Natural History of the Spanish Peninsula, states that the
potato was first brought to Europe by the Spaniards, who
introduced it to Galicia whence, via Ireland, it spread to
the rest of Europe. De Candolle, the Swiss botanist, in his
Origin of Cultivated Plants, corroborates this opinion of
Bowles.

In 1621, on the 12th and 14th of October there occurred
'The Wonderful Battell of Starelings.' In a British
Museum tract dated 1622 we read: 'About the seventh of
October last, Anno 1621 there gathered together by degrees, an unusual multitude of birds called stares, in some
Countries knowne by the name of Starlings. . . . It is
and hath beene an old proverbe, that, *Birds of a feather
hold and keep together,* which hath ever beene a common
custome in these as much as in any other kind whatsoever,
but now the old proverb is changed, and their custome is
altered cleane contrary. For at this time, as these birds are
in taste bitter, so they met to fight together the most bit-
terest and sharpest battell amongst themselves, the like,
for the manner of their fight, and for the time the battell
did continue, never heard or seene at any time in any country of the world. . . .

'Now to come to the flight of our birds, the stares or starlings, they mustered together at this above named Citie of
Corke some foure or five daies, before they fought their
battells, every day more and more encreasing their armies
with greater supplies, some came as from the East, others
from West, and so accordingly they placed themselves, and
as it were encamped themselves eastward and westward
about the citie, during which time their noise and tunes
were strange on both sides to the great admiration of the

citizens and the inhabitants near adjoining, who had never
seen for multitude, or ever heard for loud tunes which they
uttered, the like before. Whereupon they more curiously
observing the courses and passages they used, noted that
from those on the East, and from those on the West, sundry
flights, some twenty or thirty in a company, would passe
from the one side to the other, as it should seeme imployed
in embassages, for they would fly and hover in the ayre over
the adverse party with strange tunes and noise and so return
back again to that side from which as it seemed they were
sent. . . .

'These courses and customes continued with them until
the XII of October, which day being Saturday, about nine
of the clocke in the morning, being a very faire and sun-
shine day, upon a strange sound and noise made as well on
the one side as on the other, they forthwith at one instant
took wing, and so mounting up into the skyes encountered
one another, with such a terrible shocke, as the evening was
somewhat dark and the battell was fought over woods more
remote off, but for more assured proof of this fight the Sunday before named, there are at this time in London divers
persons of worth and very honest reputation, whom the
Printer of this Pamphlet can produce to justifie what they
saw, as cause shall require upon their oaths.

'Now to return to the last battell fought at Corke by
these stares. Upon Munday the XIV of October, they made
their return again, and at the same time, the day being as
faire a sun-shine day as it was the Saturday before, they
mounted into the aire and encountered each other with
like violent assaults as formerly they had done, and fell
into the citie upon the houses, and into the river, wounded
and slaughtered in like manner as before is reported, but
at this last battell there was a kite, a Raven and a Crow, all

three found dead in the streets, rent, torn and mangled.'

For some reason amongst those claiming to be intimately acquainted with the divine mind, this battle of the starlings was said to prognosticate 'the first original of the ruin of Cork,' just as, a few years before, in 1587, flocks of wild geese, fighting with each other on the confines of Croatia near Wihitzium, in Hungary, were, afterwards, said to presage the invasion of that country by the Turks. In another tract in the British Museum we find:

'A Relation of the Most Lamentable Burning of the Cittie of Corke, in the West of Ireland, in the Province of Munster, by Thunder and Lightning. . . .'

The author of this pamphlet then goes on to prove his case, at length, but as I am not in entire agreement, I will forbear further quotation, saving only his concluding sentence: 'And what the battell and fight of the birds did presage and prognosticate, fell out too true and doleful in the utter ruin and consumption of a rich and wealthy citie.'

Whatever destruction this city had suffered by this 'fire from Heaven,' it recovered sufficiently within twenty-nine years for Cromwell to come along and convert the bells of its churches into cannon for his 'protecting' army. Thirty-eight years later, in 1688, James II landed in Cork. Two years after that the city was besieged by the forces of King William.

Then we come to a more cheerful event, the foundation of the oldest yacht club in Great Britain or Ireland. Some time prior to 1720 the Cork Water Club, later 'The Royal Cork Yacht Club,' was formed. In 1748 we get the following description of the fleet under sail, from 'Two English Gentlemen' who made 'A Tour through Ireland':

'It is somewhat like that of the Doge of *Venice*'s wedding

at Sea. A Set of worthy **Gentlemen,** who have formed themfelves into a Body, which they call the *Water-Club,* proceed a few Leagues out to Sea once a Year, in a Number of little Veffels, which for Painting and Gilding exceed the King's Yachts at *Deptford* and *Greenwich.* Their Admiral, who is elected annually, and hoifts his Flag on board his little veffel, leads the Van, and receives the Honours of the Flag. The reft of the Fleet fall in their proper Stations, and keep their Line in the fame manner as the King's Ships. This Fleet is attended with a prodigious Number of Boats; which, with their Colours flying, Drums beating, and Trumpets founding, forms one of the moft agreeable and fplendid Sights your Lordfhip can conceive.'

By 1765 the club had prospered to such an extent that it became necessary to resolve 'that no admiral presume to bring more than two dozen of wine to his treat.' In 1807 it was sufficiently progressive to decide 'that the wives and daughters of the members of the club be also considered as members of the club and entitled to wear their uniform.' But possibly on account of too great zeal on the part of the new members, it became necessary, a little later, to draft a solemn resolution that, in the case of those new members, breeches will not form part of the uniform.

On 10th September 1766 a tailor by the name of Patrick Redmond was executed in Cork for robbing a dwelling-house. But after hanging for nine minutes he was cut down by his friends and perfectly restored to life 'by the dint of friction and fumigation.' Among those who helped in this kindly act was the actor Glover, then playing at the local theatre. Redmond, having made his escape, got drunk and went to the playhouse that night to thank Mr. Glover for his help, whereby the whole audience was put in terror and consternation.

During the summer of 1815 there came to a County Cork woman the following letter:

H.M.S. *Bellerophon,*
Plymouth Sound,
Sunday 30th July 1815.

MY DEAR MOTHER,

You will be surprised at not hearing from me, and knowing the *Bellerophon's* arrival in England, but when I tell you no private letters were allowed to leave the ship before to-day that will cease. It is unnecessary to say we have got Buonaparte and suite on board, as it was known in England previous to our arrival, which took place on the 24th instant in Torbay.

The circumstances which led to his surrender were his defeats in all points; and was it not for the strict blockade that was kept up would have escaped to America. We heard of his being on board the French Frigate *Saale,* off Rochefort, from which moment we watched his motions, if possible, more closely than before. On the morning of the 14th instant, observing a Schooner bearing a flag of truce on board standing towards us we hove to for her, when Count Lascazas and General Lallemande came on board with proposals from Buonaparte, in consequence of which we came to anchor in the evening off Rochelle. Next morning, 16th instant, at 4 a.m., observed a man-of-war brig standing out, and beating towards us, we immediately despatched all our boats; Lieutenant Mott, in the barge, brought Buonaparte on board at seven, the boats were busily employed bringing his retinue and luggage, and I never saw men exert themselves as much as ours did that day, lest Admiral Hotham should take him, as he was off the harbour in the *Superb,* and saw him coming on board here, and did all in his power to get in but did not come to anchor before eleven in the forenoon.

Buonaparte is a fine looking man, inclined to corpulency; is five feet six inches in height, his hair turning gray and a little bald on the crown of the head, no whiskers, complexion French yellow, eyes gray, Roman nose, good mouth and chin, neck short, big belly, arms stout, small white hands, and shows a good leg. He wears a cocked hat, something like our own three-cornered ones, with the tricoloured cockade in it, plain green coat, cape red and cuffs of the same, plain gold epaulets and a large star on the left breast, white waistcoat and breeches, and white silk stockings, thin shoes and buckles. Eats but two meals in the day, breakfast and dinner; these are sumptuous—fish, flesh and fowl, wines, fruits, various French dishes, etc., etc., he breakfasts about eleven and dines at six, is about half an hour at each, when he generally comes on deck, or goes into the after cabin to study.

We do not know what's to be done with him, yet he remains on board until we hear from the Allies. . . .

P.S. I think myself lucky to belong to the old *Bellerophon* at this important time.

Other Cork men were on board the *Bellerophon* at that time, too. There was Barry O'Meara, the ship's surgeon, who, later, accepted the emperor's invitation to remain with him in St. Helena as medical adviser. There was Lieutenant William Conner, R.N., from Ballybricken House on the shores of Cork harbour, and there was Eames Westropp, who, being the youngest officer on board, was deputed to receive Napoleon's sword.

In the year 1811 Daniel Maclise was born in Cork. While still a young man he painted four of the frescoes in the

House of Lords. Since then the British Constitution has been maintained in an aura of Cork colours.

On the 1st of April 1838 the Cork steamer *Sirius* sailed from Cork for America, the first steamer to cross the Atlantic.

On the 23rd of March 1889 who should be born in Cork but myself.

CHAPTER TWENTY-EIGHT

FOR CLOSE ON THREE MILES above Cork the river runs
slow and smooth as if reluctant to meet the sea. Pleasant meadows border the stream, meadows in a wide valley,
the gateway to the west. There are no man-made barriers
in the fields beside the Lee. If there is a fence there is also
a stile or a gate. You can walk the full length of the river
without seeing a notice board. You can walk the whole
length of its course without seeing even a village, for, from
Cork to its source, there is not a hamlet on its banks. A
house here and there, a cottage by a bridge. Such lovely
bridges, too. As you follow the banks there is just sufficient
track to give you confidence. It may be cattle or sheep, or
even rabbits, perhaps the footsteps of a labourer going to
and from his work that has tempered the growing of the
grass. The glory of the river is yours.

Three miles from the city, at Carrigrohane, the valley
narrows and the river flows beside the road close under the
castle on its high white cliff. My father was rector of Carrigrohane for twenty-two years. 'Ah, sure, there's never

been any one like the canon. Didn't he do as much for us as for his own?' said a Roman Catholic to me. 'And wouldn't he be down on his knees on the cottage floors playing with the children? Sure he couldn't pass the door without giving them a sweet.' Rich and poor, Protestant and Catholic alike, loved him. Even if he did believe, as I have heard him say from the pulpit, that the devil was waiting outside the church door like a black cat ready to jump on our shoulders as we went out, his sincerity was, in itself, an inspiration. His was the simplest, most innocent nature. I remember how shocked and hurt he was, one time in London, when having lost his ticket on the underground, he was compelled to pay another twopence. He that could have travelled from one end of Ireland to another and back again on his word alone.

'I wouldn't get a letter in ten years,' said Jerry Linehan, when, after thirty years, I met him on Carrigrohane bridge, 'and all of a sudden there was one on the table before me, and I runs the knife through it, and the first thing I sees is your name. Wisha, Master Bob, Mister Bob, what'll I call you after all these years? Wisha, Bob, when I seen your name it took twenty years off me life. Do you remember the day we had at Coolineagh? You had your pointer bitch with you, and the first thing you did was to fall into the bog down to your belly. And then you shot a brace of duck and we couldn't find either of them, and then you got a teal, and after that we had the hell of a day after snipe, and then you says to me, you says: "Jerry, will we miss the train?" "We will," says I, and with that we got another few snipe, and then you got another couple of duck and the last one had a clutch of eggs under her, for 'twas late in the season and she was early, and then we found the two you'd shot in the morning, and then we had fifteen miles

before us to walk and we tramping since nine o'clock in
the morning and the bag full. "We'll get a horse and car,"
says you; but divil a horse and car could we get. "My father
will surely send the pony and trap to meet us," says you;
but divil a pony or trap to meet us. And the eggs was in
my pockets and one of them was broken and we had every
inch of fifteen miles before us. And your father was raging
mad when we got in. " 'Tis tame ducks you're after stran-
gling," said he, "and 'tis four hours back you ought to
have been in," he said. And the next morning your sister
comes along to me, and I was in bed for I couldn't get up.
"How are you, Jerry?" says she. "I'm all right in the head,"
says I, "but the legs are gone from me, and the feet under
me," I says, "if I could put 'em under me wouldn't stay
under me." And 'twas two days before I could put the
boots on me again. And all the eggs but the broken one
in me trousers pocket hatched out, and the little wild
duckeens were waddling round the haggard up at the rectory till all of a sudden the call comes to them and never
again were they seen.'

We dropped into the 'Angler's Rest' near by, just to sit
down. 'Do you remember the morning we went shooting
rabbits among the major's milch cows and he reported us
to your father? And your father says to me, "Jerry," he
says, "what are you doing taking my son shooting rabbits
among the major's milch cows?" He was carrying an armful of parcels up from the station for old Mother Burke at
the time. And says I to him: "Would you have me take
him shooting among a herd of milch bulls?" "Jerry," says
he, "there's no correcting you." And do you remember
Paddy Regan and the way he was caught at the poaching?
Out in the morning, early, he'd been, and a couple of nice
salmon he'd brought back. Hid them in the hayrick in the

haggard he did. And when the police came along there was Paddy sitting up at his breakfast, rubbing the sleep out of his eyes, as innocent as you please. Every inch of his house they searched and not a sign of a scale. But what did they see as they were going down the lane from the house, only Paddy's two cats, and they with the fish between them. Dragged them out of the hayrick, they did. Twenty pounds it cost him. He couldn't bear the sight of a cat ever after.'

Along the main road from Cork there ran, until a few years ago, the Cork and Muskerry Light Railway. Its station was immediately under the big cliff, and the station-master, Dan Corcoran, was a particular friend of mine. For years Dan had been an exemplary official, a model servant of the company. He was punctual, sober, efficient, polite, never even asked for a rise in pay. But trouble came to him, and it was like this. One day he was wrongfully accused of having started a fight at a hurley match. The accuser was the guard on the railway, and he told the engine-driver. Both guard and engine-driver belonged to the district whose team had been beaten at the match. Every time that the train passed through Carrigrohane station, and it must have been nearly a dozen times in the day, both guard and driver shouted taunts at Corcoran, asking him why he had started the row. Shouted them for all to hear.

Wrongful accusations are some of the hardest things to bear, but Corcoran bore them all that day, bore, too, the inquiring looks of passengers who heard those taunts. He bore them all, he, the quietest of men on earth, until the last train was going out of the station that evening. Then he jumped into the van. He hit the guard one stroke on the chin that put him senseless on the floor of the van, and then he jumped out of the train on the other side.

After that he went back and locked up the station. He handed in the keys to the post office, and he went home. He told them at the post office that they could do what they liked with the keys, that he was finished with the railway.

Of course, the directors of the railway did not like the idea of their trains going along the line without a guard; so, independently, they came to the same decision as Dan, that he *had* finished with the railway. My father was the only one who was really worried by the whole proceeding, for the guard recovered in a couple of days. Father did not like to see Dan lose his job. Therefore he paid a visit to Cork, and he persuaded the directors that an apology from Dan would put everything right. But Dan could see no reason to apologize. What was there to apologize for? Let the guard do the apologizing, if that was what was wanted. Thus, Dan was out of work.

In spite of my regrets this suited my own book very well, for though I had not resorted to such extreme measures, I also was having trouble with my directors, the professors at the college. It wasn't that there was any ill will between us, it was just that they couldn't agree with my answers to their questions. The professor of zoology lamented that I seemed more interested in the outside than the inside of a rabbit. While, then, I was endeavouring to persuade my relations that a graver was more suited to my temperament than a scalpel Dan and I had plenty of days and nights to wander by the river, through bogs, or over hills. I do not remember anything spectacular about those days. It is little things that come to my memory, like the crunch of frosted snow under our feet, or the balancing along an ice-covered pole across a stream at night, or the waiting in ambush for duck, knowing that there was also a large bull in the same field. There were, too, the flocks of golden plover that would sometimes sweep across the sky, a dark filigree, a veil, a cloud of wings forming and re-forming, swinging here, circling there, leaders ever changing, suddenly accelerating, as suddenly dropping almost to earth, a rain of silver. And the early drives to get to the bogs at daybreak, with Dan and the spaniel on one side of the outside car, and myself with the pointer on the other side, and Johnny Kinneally, the driver, holding in a horse that trotted up steep hills as fast as it trotted down their other side.

And I mustn't forget the boat that we built, and how the salmon fishers hated us for it. It afterwards became the roof of a hen-house near the mouth of Cork harbour. It was the second of my efforts at boat-building. The first, hardly more than a canoe, I decided, for privacy's sake, to keep hidden under the flood arch of a stream. But, unknown to me, some gentlemen who used nets at night also sheltered in that same arch, and, when they found my boat, as it were offered to them, they gladly availed themselves of its services and I never saw it again.

But the final episode of my gun must be told. It began in 1915 when, before going to the Dardanelles, I gave it to Dan Corcoran, with instructions that he was to hold on to it until I asked him for it again. If by chance I did not come back, he was to keep it. I did come back, but as I was then living in England I had no need to reclaim the weapon. It was, therefore, still in his possession when the 'troubles' began in Ireland. As things grew worse I tried to get messages through, telling him to hand in the gun to the authorities. But he had not done so when the death penalty was announced for any one found in possession of fire-arms. Again and again I sent him messages. Occasionally I would get a reply that he didn't care a damn for the military or the death penalty: he would hand my gun to no one but myself. In this way weeks and months went on. At last I got a written note to him, saying that he must get rid of the weapon, somehow, I didn't care how. A fortnight later I had a postcard: 'Very sorry, had to drown the dog last week.'

Even then he had 'one last bit of sport.' The military barracks were immediately opposite the door of his cottage. At the far side of the drill field there was a canal. This was the place selected for the rite. Taking the gun from its hiding place in the rafters, in the full light of day, he divided the barrel from the stock. Then inside each leg of his trousers he put one piece. Thus accoutred he sauntered past the sentries, strolled through the recreation grounds, went and had a look at the troops on parade, chatted with soldiers off duty, and passed on through the horse lines down to the canal. Then, while apparently sitting on the bank, watching fish, he straightened out his legs and let the two parts of the gun slide quietly into the water.

CHAPTER TWENTY-NINE

ABOVE CARRIGROHANE the Lee is merry and sparkling. In its course it has not yet given way to the sedateness, almost solemnity that it assumes nearer to the city. There is a sprightliness, a spring-like gaiety in its flow, even when the red leaves, argonauts of autumn, swirl, and are carried from pool to pool. Its first important tributary, the Shournagh, joins it here, a small stream tumbling and twisting through a wooded valley. That stream flows beside a village as famous as the city of Carthage, Pompeii, or Thebes. What city, town, or village in the world has given its name as noun and verb to the English or any other language? Only one; the village of Blarney.

Cities of the world depend for their fame on piles of stones, scattered or in order, but this village, where naught but tweeds are made, rests all its fame upon a single stone. That stone is in the parapet of the castle, Blarney Castle, built in the fifteenth century by Cormac MacCarthy, whose genealogy will be found in Keating's *History of Ireland,* ascending through Heber the Fair, son of Milesius, the Spanish hero, up to the patriarch Noah himself, not a link in the chain missing.

On arrival at the castle, the pilgrim climbs to its battlemented summit, and having handed any loose valuables that might be in his pockets to a friend, lowers himself head first between parapet and main building. Thus he is able

(182)

to add one more kiss to that stone already highly polished by the lips of votaries.

Although the present owner of the castle has very kindly put iron bars for the convenience of visitors it is nevertheless wise to have at least two friends holding on to your shins during the operation. Not that anything very serious can happen. The last man who fell, eighty feet into the tree below, was able to report for duty next day.

The power of the stone was first made known to Cormac the Strong, the builder of the castle, who, being a bit worried about a lawsuit in which, even in those early days, he had become embroiled, was wandering, moody, in the adjacent forest. There he met Cliodhna, the 'Queen of the Fairies.' 'I'll tell you what it is,' said she. 'Don't vex yourself any more. Go home to your bed,' said she, 'and lie down and sleep, and in the morning, at dawn, get up and go out, and right before you, facing you,' she said, 'you'll see a stone that has been brought from the banks of the Lee. Kiss it,' said she, 'kiss it, and you'll never want for words.' Cormac did as he was told, though it was a cold and a wet morning when he had to rise out of his bed. And when he went before the judge the words poured out of him like the Shournagh itself in flood. Up to the top of the castle he carried that stone, and out under the battlement he put it, for fear another would reach it, and there it is to this day.

Like many others, the castle was stormed by Cromwell. Its subsequent history may be learned from the last few lines of a popular ballad:

'He gave the estate to the Jeffers,
    With the dairy, the cows, and the hay,
And they lived there in clover like heifers,
    As their ancestors do to this day.'

It is possible that there are other stones beside the Lee with properties similar to the one in the castle. It is possible that houses have been built upon them. It is probable that one at least is the starting point of Teigue O'Leary's travels. Teigue lives in a cottage overlooking the Lee. He is a far-travelled man, in imagination. Actually he has never been outside County Cork. He is a huge, powerful man who could do the work of two ordinary labourers in the day if he had a mind to it, but, for the most part, he prefers to take things more easily. His large head is bald save for one long, wild wisp of gray hair that stands out from his forehead. He looks at you in an almost frighteningly solemn way, staring maybe at your chin or your collar or your waist-line. You feel that he is being disturbingly critical. He has a habit of getting his tongue behind his teeth and moving them from side to side in his mouth and sometimes outside of it. Apart from these disconcerting actions he is simple as a child. His smile will suddenly burst upon you like the light through an opened door.

For many years he acted as gillie to fishermen on the river, and many of those fishermen were retired sailors and soldiers. There were two, in particular, that stuck in Teigue's mind, the captain and the general. 'The general was great gas altogether. He had a belly on him like a fat goose. The captain was that thin you'd mistake him for his own fishing-rod.' From these and other travellers Teigue would hear of the world beyond the Irish Sea, and he would question them again and again, and then he would go home in the evening and tell his wife, Maggie, a quiet, dark-haired little woman, all that he had heard. And the two of them would sit together by the fire, and they would go backwards and forwards over the stories, and gradually Teigue would come to believe that he had been in those places. His mind had never once strayed from Maggie, though he liked to tease her with stories of his adventures. She, knowing how much to believe, would play up to him accordingly.

'Were 'oo ever in Paris?' he would ask a visitor. 'Isn't it the grand city? I went to the Follies. What is it you call them? The Folly-bare-something?'

'Bare everything,' suggests Maggie.

'Me and Patsy Ryan went in and when the screen was drawn wasn't there twenty girls on the platform and they dressed up as swans. Faith it wasn't five minutes before the divil of a wind comes in and blows all the feathers off of them.'

'And what had they on?' asks Maggie.

'They hadn't a pocket handkerchief between the twenty of them.'

'And had they nothing on at all?'

'Jewels,' said Teigue.

'And what were they doing?'

'Faith, then, I don't know what they were doing, but 'twas very queer doin' whatever it was.'

'And where else did ye go?'

'We went to Rome.'

'Did ye see the pope?'

'We did not. He was busy the day we were there.'

'Sure, he must have an awful lot to do,' says Maggie. 'Were ye ever in India?'

'We were, of course.'

'And what is it like?'

'Yerra, 'tis all palaces, and elephants and alligators.'

'And were ye in London?'

'We were to be sure.'

'Did ye see Buckingham Palace?'

'We did.'

'And what is it like?'

'The floors are that slippery you couldn't walk on them without nails in your boots.'

'Isn't it a queer thing,' said Maggie, 'I like to be hearing about the kings and the castles, and they tell me the kings and the peoples in the castles do like to be reading about the people in the cottages.'

In a pool of the river just below Teigue's house, as indeed in many other parts of the Lee, the pearl-bearing freshwater mussel is to be found in abundance. There is nothing unique in that. Most of the rivers and many lakes in the mountainous coastal districts of Ireland have yielded pearls, some of them of considerable size, though of inferior lustre. In the year A.D. 1094 Gilbert, Bishop of Limerick, presented a pearl found in the Shannon to Anselm, Archbishop of Canterbury, for his mitre. In 1635 the Earl of Cork tells in his diary of 'a veary lardge rownde fine pearle' that was found in the River Bandon. The woman that found it had 'sold it in Cork for 2s. in money and 4d. in beer and tobackoe; that partie sowld it again for two cows, who sowld it the third time for £12 sterling.'

Many of the freshwater pearls found in medieval times were used in ecclesiastical decorations, especially on the bindings of missals and other manuscripts. None of them can compare for lustre with those taken from the true pearl-oyster. In Britain freshwater pearls have been known for over 2,000 years, frequent references to them being found in Roman writings of the first and second centuries. Suetonius, in his *Lives of the Caesars,* after speaking of the admiration which Julius Caesar had for pearls, states that their occurrence in Britain was an important factor in inducing the first Roman invasion of that country in 55 B.C. Pliny (Philemon Holland's translation, 1601) says: 'Julius Caesar (late Emperor of famous memorie) doth not dissemble that the cuirace or breastplate which he dedicated to Venus' mother within her temple was made of English pearles.'

In the seventeenth century the White Cart river at Paisley was famous for the 'fineness' of its pearls, while those from the Irton in Cumberland were so noted that 'fair as Irton pearls' became a saying in the north country. Rivers in France, Silesia, Siberia, India, and North America have all yielded similar jewels.

Talking of Venus; with regret, a disillusionment. Cleopatra did not dissolve a pearl in wine for Antony's sake. She couldn't have done so because pearls are neither soluble in wine nor in vinegar, unless first pulverized. That would have been a difficult operation at table. If she had attempted to crush it under her heel the implications might not have been all that she desired.

CHAPTER THIRTY

FROM UNDER SHADOWY WOODS dark waters move. Silent and smooth they run, into the sunlight. Converging currents swirl in lingering eddies. That which has passed, disdainful, returns to dally. Reflections rippling in the pools laugh at their own staid parents on the bank.

Above the long bridge with its many arches, and opposite the old church at Inniscarra, the tributary, Bride, joins the Lee. A wild stream from the south, it takes its name from the fifteenth-century monastery, dedicated to St. Brigid, which stands on its banks. In the nave of that abbey is the tomb of Arthur O'Leary, the 'outlaw,' a victim of that fantastic religious persecution that continued for over a hundred years in Ireland and lasted well into the nineteenth century. During that time no dignitary of the Roman Catholic Church might remain in Ireland. No Roman Catholic had the right of franchise, municipal or parliamentary. No one of that religion could become a barrister

(188)

or solicitor, or enter the army. No schools or colleges of that religion were allowed in the country. A Protestant heiress who married a Roman Catholic was deprived of her estates. The eldest son of a Roman Catholic could, by changing his religion, make his own father a mere tenant on his estate. A Roman Catholic was not allowed even to own a horse worth more than five pounds. If he did, a Protestant, tendering that sum to him, could compel him to sell, however valuable that animal might be.

Arthur O'Leary had served with distinction in the Hungarian Army in the latter part of the eighteenth century, retiring with the rank of major. When he returned to Ireland he brought with him his charger, and this horse he would sometimes ride to hounds. One day, after a long and hard ride with the Muskerry hunt, he 'took the brush.' Thereupon a Mr. Morris, a magistrate, rode up and, tendering five pounds, claimed the horse. O'Leary said that he would sooner part with his life. Morris summarily declared him an outlaw. Soldiers were sent out, and within a few days O'Leary was shot dead when on his way to his home.

It was these travesties of justice that turned the Irish people 'agin the Government.' They came to know it only as an enemy, as the instrument of injustice rather than of justice. It may seem hard to some people, unacquainted with Irish history as written by Irishmen, to believe the testimony of Sir John Davies, an Englishman, Attorney-General for Ireland under James I, that 'there is no nation of people under the sunne that doth love equal and indifferent justice better than the Irish; or will rest better satisfied with the execution thereof, although it bee against themselves; so as they may have the protection and benefit of the law, when upon just cause they do desire it.' Yet that only corroborates the whole tenor of Irish literature, whether legendary, legal, or historical, that the Irish of olden times held truth to be the highest of the virtues, and obeyed a law gladly, supported by no other force than public opinion.

After Inniscarra the hills gather closely, and the river laughs out loud. It dances, it prances, it rushes, it slides, calm for a moment then onward again, stream racing stream, leaping and tumbling, wild Bacchanalian, wine from the mountains, froth from the ecstasy blown through the reeds. Mile after mile, past larch woods and beech woods and fern-covered hillsides, castles, and 'standing stones' cresting high ground. In comes the torrent from wild Knockabrocka, bringing turf waters from Aghabullogue; down comes the water from Carriganish.

Twelve miles from Inniscara to Carrigadrohid, with its fourteenth-century castle in the middle of the river. Twelve miles of silver-stepped fountains. So flows this river unsullied by a town.

A few miles from the main stream, on the Sullane, stands Carrigaphooka Castle; Carrigaphooka, the Rock of the Púca, or spirit. Isolated on its rocky foundations, with walls a span thick, it dominates the valley. And more than mortal agencies are at work for its protection. Many a tale is told of the 'court' that is held within its walls after midnight and of the misadventures of intruding mortals.

Now the Lee comes to us in a wide network of interlacing streams, the 'Gearagh,' haunt of the wild duck, home of the ring-dove. Water swirling by a thousand wooded islets; under the overhanging fern-laden, moss-covered oaks; under the alders and hazels; through tangles of rushes, swaying tall weeds; through tortuous channels, trailing long grasses; an almost impenetrable jungle, certainly one in which the most knowledgeable man might lose his way. 'Twas here that Shawn Ruadh hid after he had been declared an outlaw for taking part in one of the Whiteboy risings about the year 1770. 'Shawn Ruadh Gearagh,' he was called—Red-haired John of the Gearagh. Many were the unsuccessful attempts to find him. They even put bloodhounds on to his trail, and one of them did track Shawn to the hollow tree in which he lived. Shawn was about to cook a bit of meat when he saw the hound coming. Quickly he fixed it on the point of his sword and held it for a moment in the fire to heighten its smell. When the hound came up Shawn held out the red meat to it. The animal couldn't resist. As it took the flesh from the sword Shawn drove the weapon deep into the animal's throat and killed it. There was no sound to give away his hiding-place. Many other stories have been told before that of the final incident in the chase. In that, Shawn had crept past the guards to a house where the magistrate

and the military officers were sitting at a table playing cards
by the light of a candle. Through the open window Shawn
fired a shot that blew out the candle 'just to show them that
he could have killed them if he had wanted to.' Whether
it was in admiration of his shooting or in apprehension of
further marksmanship we are not told but, because he
didn't kill them, he was given a pardon, and from that
time on went free.

Again the river flows as a single stream, its course between rich pastures. On either side, on almost every hill
there stands some relic of the past, ancient earthworks,
standing stones, or castles. Many of the earthworks are
simple in form, a bank and a ditch to enclose the home-
stead; others, with their more complicated ramparts, were,
plainly, intended for defence; others again were probably
for ceremonies of the clan.

Single standing stones, known as gallauns, are everywhere. There must be thousands of them in County Cork
alone. Some may be inconspicuous, no taller than the sheep
that graze beside them, others, like the great pillar at Bally-
vourney, may be more than three times the height of a
tall man. Dating from neolithic times, they appear to have
been used for at least three different purposes: as memorials to the dead, to mark the site of some great battle, or
to establish a boundary. For the most part they have no
markings on them other than those carved by the forces
of nature; they are simple unchiselled slabs or pillars. But
a few, and those by far the most interesting, have inscrip-
tions cut in what is known as the Ogham alphabet, a form
of lettering composed of lines or groups of lines, a few
inches in length, cut across or on either side of a median
line, such as the edge of a stone. Of necessity the inscrip-
tions were short, usually not more than the name of the

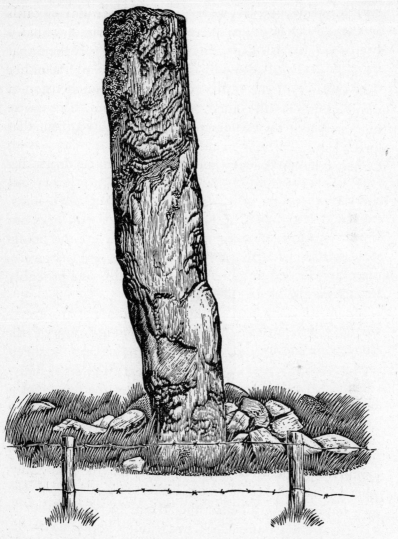

dead man and that of his father: 'Fiachra son of Glunleg-
get,' or 'Cluicunas son of Mactrenos.'

Only about four hundred of these memorials, in all, are
known, and of that number some fifty are in Great Britain.

Of the remainder the vast majority come from the south of Ireland, particularly the counties of Kerry, Cork, and Waterford, all of them in the very earliest form of Irish. Their date would seem to be from about the middle of the fifth century to the latter part of the seventh century, though there is still controversy on this point. It has been suggested that their character arose from an alphabet of finger signs. Early Irish manuscripts tell of messages in Ogham cut on pieces of wood and sent from one important

person to another, much as message sticks are sent among primitive people to-day. These stones may be found anywhere. One that I came across, hitherto unchronicled, was in a loose stone wall near the Mizen Head. Another at Kilbrittain, in County Cork, was leaning against a cottage. 'What are you doing with that stone?' I asked. 'Putting it in the rockery,' I was told. 'Put it in a museum,' I said, 'where it belongs.' They agreed. When I lifted it to make a drawing I found a cross carved on its under side, proving either that Ogham writing was contemporary with Christianity or that the stone was a pagan monument converted, at a later date, to Christian uses.

Seven miles short of Inchigeela the hollow shell of Droumcarra Castle may be seen on the side of a hill. Five miles nearer to the village Carrignacurra Castle, in better repair, stands guarding a ford. There, one night in every year, an O'Leary comes to seek his wife of long ago. Against all her entreaties he had joined in a rising, promising to be with her again on a certain night. Before that night came he was killed in battle. Now through the centuries he keeps his tryst.

CHAPTER THIRTY~ONE

AT INCHIGEELA the character of the country changes
abruptly. No longer the swift river among broad
meadows; now it is wide lakes and wild moorland, with
crowded mountain peaks on all horizons. I spent a day on
those lakes in early September. The boat was a small one,
so short that it was almost circular, and it had but two
seats, one in the bow and the other in the stern. If I sat in
the stern the bow went up in the air and the water lapped
the gunwale beside me. If I sat in the bow it was the stern

that reared itself like the quarter of a fifteenth-century caravel.

'Stay where you are now, till I get a few stones,' said Teigue, the owner of the boat, as I balanced in the bow. He went to a wall and brought back a large boulder. 'You should have been here for the regatta,' he said, as he lifted it on to the stern seat. 'Paddy Jack Murphy and Paddy Tim Casey had the hell of a fine race. Paddy Jack had a sailor from Bantry in the boat with him, and Paddy Tim had a guarda from Macroom, and the two pairs of them was old rivals.'

Teigue went for another stone. When he came back he continued the story.

'The two boats were below at the start waiting for the gun when all of a sudden Paddy Jack and the sailor started rowing. "Go on. What's keeping ye?" yelled the crowd at Paddy Tim. "We're waiting for the shot," said Paddy Tim. "Yerra never mind the shot, the gun is stuck." With that Paddy Tim and the guarda started. You never saw such rowing in your life. They lifted the boat out of the water with the dint of their strokes, and they won the race.'

Teigue collected some more stones, piled them in the stern, and pushed me from the bank. The gunwale was about four inches above the water. It seemed much less.

The narrow stream, whence I sailed, soon widened into the lake. The boat moved with the current. The surface of the lake was like glass. Rich, lowland fields, backed by heather-clad hills, were mirrored in the water. Corn stooks stood on their own reflections. The edge of the lake was carpeted with white lilies. Mallard rose from a fringe of weeds. A man in a white jacket, with two black horses at the plough, was turning the green velvet of a field into brown furrows.

Faint whiffs of breeze rippled the water, lifting the edges of the lily leaves. Grey clouds were gathering on the hills to the west. While I stopped to make a drawing the wind increased. Squalls hit the lake and water splashed over the gunwale. I landed to shelter under a holly-tree while a shower swept across the valley. A man came and spoke to me. I asked him if he knew the time. He said: 'What with new time and old time and God's time it is hard to say what time it is.' He took from his pocket the works of a clock. 'It will be midday, just, by old time, but that's half an hour ahead of the sun,' he said. Then we talked for a while, and he asked: 'Are you the man is writing a book?'

'I am,' I said.

'Have you seen the Mass Rock, where they said mass when the priests was hunted?'

'I have not.'

'Come, and I'll show it to you.'

We followed the road for about half a mile, to where, under a low cliff, we found this relic of penal times, rough slabs of stone built to form an altar. 'Mass was said here 1640–1800' was inscribed on a metal disk beside it.

'Yerra there's lots of them about the country,' he said. 'There's one west at Coomataggart and there's another three miles to the south at Kilnadur. Tell me,' he added, 'did I see you with your shirt off in the boat?'

'You probably did.'

' 'Tis the best in the world for the rheumatics. There was a man east there beyond Clonmoyle, and he doubled up in the bed and unable to move. And the priest comes in to him, and he says: "Will you do what I tell you," he says. "I will," he said. "Go out in the sun," says the priest, "and let it roast ye." Faith a March hare couldn't catch him ever since.'

Back in the boat, the lake was calm again. I couldn't help thinking of those rough altars and of all that they implied, and the curious fact that when peoples or individuals inflict great injury on their fellow creatures they generally do so believing their actions to be right. Even Cromwell thought himself to be an instrument of God. To-day the same is happening, not only in the wider spheres of life, but in our private lives. Right and wrong can be so easily defined to ourselves by what we would like to be right and wrong. It is difficult to disentangle self-interest from our politics.

Now the wind was rising again, and the lake was being whipped to silver. Wind and water were joined in wisps of spray, and waves were again coming on board. Glints of sunlight lit the cornfields, as a match flares and fades. A cormorant, so black, flew across the lake. Fifteen pounds of fish is the normal daily consumption of one of these birds.

But I was getting wet, and it became a question of me or the stones. I gave the stones the honour. Over the side they went, and up went the stern. There was just clearance when I knelt amidships. And so I sailed into shelter.

'Begod 'twas on a tea-tray I thought you were,' said a man to me, as I stepped ashore.

It was on a road through this valley, to the north, that, one night, a man by the name of Patsy Kerrigan was on his way home. He was walking fast for there was a chill on the night, and, as he went, he came upon three men, and they carrying a coffin. Thinking to help them he took the fourth place, but no sooner had his shoulder touched the wood than the three men let down the coffin on the road and disappeared. It seemed strange to Patsy. He waited a while, and a while longer, hoping they would return, but no sight or sign of them coming back. And there he was on the road, alone, with a coffin. After a while he remembered a cottage near by, where friends of his lived. So, leaving the coffin where they'd put it, he went along to his friends and he told them what had happened. They didn't know what to think of it either, for none of them knew of any one that was after dying. But they went along with Patsy, and the coffin was there on the road. And after a while they unscrewed the lid, and they opened it, and inside was a foxy-haired girl. And it seemed as if she mightn't be dead at all, for she was sweating. So they lifted her out and they took her home and, sure enough, by next morning she was able to talk to them. And she told them who she was and who were her parents and where she came from. So Patsy and one of the men in the cottage went off to tell her father, and when they found him he was digging spuds in the field below his house, and he wouldn't believe them. 'My daughter is above in the bed, sick, this fortnight,' he said. Still and all, he went and had a look at her, and she was there in the bed right enough. So they had great trouble in persuading the father to go with them. But, in the latter end, he went, and, as sure as he did, it was his daughter that he found before him. You may say he was puzzled. But there was no doubt about it at all. There could be no mistake. So he took her home with him. And when he got home he took her into the bedroom, and the bed was empty. The other girl had gone. She was a changeling, d'you see. So the girl that was rescued married the man that was after taking her from the fairies, and she was sister to the grand-mother of Dan Clancy who told me this.

On the other side of the lakes, in the hills to the south, there was a man by the name of Kelleher, and his wife died, and one night, a year after she died, he was in bed, in the settle-bed in the kitchen where he used to sleep, and he saw her come in and sit down at the table where she used to sit. But she said nothing. And after a while she got up and she went out. And the next night she came again, and she sat down again, and she went out again without ever a word. So the third night he prepared a meal for her and laid it on the table for her, and she came in again and she sat down in the same seat. But she never touched the meal. She didn't say a word to him, and he didn't say a word to her until, when he saw her getting up to go out, he jumped in front of her and stood in the door before her.

'Don't touch me! Don't touch me!' she said. 'Don't touch me at all!' she said.

'What can I do for you?' he said. 'Is there anything at all I can do for you?'

'There is,' she said, 'and if you want to save me you must do as I tell you. To-morrow night,' she said, 'I'll be passing in a procession of horsemen, and I'll be up on a black horse, behind a man. You must have a ring of mountain ash on the road, with the bark peeled off, and the bare twigs sprinkled with holy water. And you must have a March cock inside, made fast with a string to your leg.' (A March cock is a bird from an egg laid and hatched in March.) 'And when you see me you must make a spring at me, and lift me down from the horse into the middle of the ring of ash, without you ever touching the horse, or the rider that's on it, or me touching a twig of the ash. And you must hold me tightly,' she said, 'when you've got a hold of me. And if you do that you'll save me.'

So Kelleher did as he was told, and he was there with the circle of ash on the road, with the bark peeled, and it all sprinkled with holy water, and the procession came along, and there was his wife, up behind another fellow, on the back of a dark slippery horse. When he seen her he made a spring at her, and he lifted her right into the circle of twigs, and no sooner did her feet touch the ground than the cock crew. And when they looked around them there wasn't a sight of the procession or the ash-twigs. So the two of them went home together, and she bore three children to him in the years that came after.

CHAPTER THIRTY-TWO

At Ballingeary the Lee changes again. The wide-spreading lakes have gone. Now it is a mountain torrent, cascading over natural weirs, sluicing under rocks, lingering a moment, then whirling on again. On all sides boulder-strewn moor, heather and gorse, holly, rowan, and birch, royal ferns, meadow-sweet, and broom.

Ballingeary is the friendliest village in the world. Every one knows every one and all about every one. For anything you want there is always someone who knows someone who can manage it for you.

The village once boasted a very famous doctor. 'There wasn't the equal of him in London, and he had two hounds and there wasn't the equal of them in Ireland. And one day he was out with the two hounds, and they put up a hare and away they went out of sight and never stopped till the three of them fell stretched outside a cottage near Fermoy, and that's fifty miles away. And the doctor was behind in Ballingeary, and he not knowing where the divil were his dogs. So the man in the cottage came out, and he seen the two hounds stretched, but he never seen the hare. And he took the hounds into the cottage and gave them milk and eggs, and with that he brought them back to life. And the next day what did he see in the paper but a reward of fifty pounds for the two dogs. 'Twas the doctor in Ballingeary was after offering it. But they were the grandest pair of dogs the man at Fermoy had ever seen and he couldn't bring himself to part with them. And the next day it was a reward of a hundred pounds that was offered, and the day after that it was two hundred. "I must take them back," says he to his wife, "and get the two hundred." But his son says to him, he says: "Let us have one run with them before you take them back." So the two of them, the father and the son, took the hounds out on to the mountain, and they were there no time before they put up a hare, and wasn't it the selfsame hare and didn't she lead the two hounds back to Ballingeary, and didn't the doctor find the three of them stretched before his door in the evening. So the fellow at Fermoy lost his two hundred pounds.'

Five miles above Ballingeary Gougane (pronounced Googawn) is reached, Gougane Barra, a valley withdrawn, a garden enclosed, the holiest place I know. Here, by this quiet pool, where, for a thousand years, tired souls have prayed, there is the peace that passes understanding. Mountains on all sides rise twelve hundred feet above the lake, forming a vast amphitheatre whose floor is silver. Small emerald fields dot the margin of the lake. Above them gigantic boulders split from the purple hills pile high. Above those boulders cliff upon cliff.

St. Finnbarr, son of Amargein, a master smith, was born near Bandon in County Cork about the year 560. At baptism he was given the name Luan, but later became known as Fionn Barr, meaning the fair-haired. From his earliest days he desired only to become a priest, and it was here at Gougane on this now flower-fringed island in the lake that in later years he built his first hermitage.

Whereas the earliest lives of the saint, one in Latin and the other in Irish, are austere in the telling, the later Irish versions, with their accumulated legends, are less restrained. In these we find references to 'miracles beyond reckoning' that were wrought by the saint. There was, for instance, the chief who, having heard of Finnbarr's miraculous powers, came to him and said: 'Were I, with my own eyes, to see some wonder performed, I would believe in your God.' And even as he spoke, though it was yet springtime, ripe nuts fell from the hazel-tree under which they were standing. Whereupon the chief believed and, kneeling, was baptized. Another time, when a neighbouring chief confiscated the land belonging to his monastery, the saint prayed to God and the land became barren. The chief then abandoned that which he had stolen, and Finnbarr, asking the blessing of God, sowed wheat therein. But, strange to relate, before the wheat came up the barley that had been planted by the robber chief not only sprouted but yielded a heavy harvest so that the saint reaped a double crop. And it is told that for twelve days after the death of 'Bairri' the sun was not darkened by clouds, and that a golden ladder was seen to rise from his church up to the gate of heaven for the souls of the faithful to ascend.

But even in our own time miracles may happen at the well. I myself know children who were sleepless, fretful, and tossing throughout the night until their mother took them to the well and bathed their eyes in its water. Ever after they slept without waking throughout the hours of darkness. I know a woman who, in this same year in which I write, went to the well one evening and prayed for a relative who was at the point of death. She came back happy and went to bed calm, for the well had bubbled. Next morning she learnt that at the very moment that the well had bubbled the sick person had taken a sudden turn for the better. And there was forty miles between them.

On the last Sunday in September, Gougane Sunday, masses are said in the oratory, and pilgrims come from far and near. In Daimler motors, in turf lorries, in the long, red-shafted country carts, in pony traps, on horseback. Those who live near travel on foot, and many from far, too. Not only by road, but over the mountains they come, strings of them climbing down the hillsides, their faces and white feet glinting like the sparkle of waterfalls. From Kilgarvan, seven miles to the north, they trickle down the slopes of Coom-ruadh; from Lackavane and Curraghglass, two miles to the south, they cross in over

Maolagh; from the west they climb whence the eagles once nested.

Besides attending mass they make their rounds at 'the stations.' Religious medals, buttons, scraps of cloth or paper, and many other oddments are left as votive offerings on the shrines or fastened to the thorn-trees. 'Praying sticks,' light twigs notched with a knife to mark each prayer, may be seen beside the shrines. Some of the penitents, in lieu of rosaries, change small stones from one hand to the other. It calls to mind those early desert fathers, Macarius the younger and Paul the Hermit, who, that they might keep reckoning of their three hundred prayers each day, collected that number of pebbles in the morning and cast one aside at the completion of each prayer.

Day after day I climb the hills. Heather and heath, heath and heather, cotton-grass, loosestrife, and myrtle. Lichens on the rocks, exquisite minute chalices dusted with silver, and miniature ivory antlers crested with crimson, springing through the stellate moss. Stars of the butterwort and clusters of London pride in the crannies. Dark pools whose lights shine blue. Bogs deep with sphagnum moss, peat-forming pockets in the groins of the hills. With each step upward a wider horizon. So it should be with life; our outlook ever widening towards the infinite rather than narrowing to the vanishing point of our own identities. And from the summits, vistas of sea and land, of infinite cloud-spread sky. Here one may walk and hear a voice that tells of order in a seeming chaos.

There is a way of quick descent for those who like such forms of travel. Six hundred feet of water-worn, moss-grown boulders, piled one on another in the innermost recess of a sunless chasm. Stepping on the moss you do not know whether your feet will find support or go through into one of the many crevices between the stones. Stepping on the bare rock, or where it is green with weed, there is little hope of anything but a sudden slide. There are drops, there are jumps, there are ledges for quiet meditation. At the foot of the 'staircase' you find yourself in the Poul, a cavernous combe where badgers and foxes make their homes, and from the Poul one hears across the 'Green Valley' the first music of the Lee. Like white veins in marble the small streams descend. Eastward the rivulet flows.

From the path beside the river, two men are visible on the crest of the hill towards the north. One of them is being lowered over a precipice on a rope to rescue a sheep. It is part of a mountainy man's job.

Across a calm stretch of the stream a few stones have been thrown. They might be a rough weir or they might be stepping-stones. But there's one gap wider than the others, and, sometimes, of a night, a sack is fastened there with its mouth held open by a stick. Fish frightened higher up will run downstream. It may not be the highest form of sport, but old men living on ten shillings a week grow hungry.

Peat stacks stand by the side of the track. They are thatched as hayricks are thatched to protect them from the weather. A donkey, hobbled, grazes by the side of the road.

'Did you know,' I said to a man, 'that donkeys only came into Ireland in the nineteenth century?'

'There's many of them must wish they'd never come, with the way they're treated,' he replied.

It must be surprising to many people to learn that from careful researches made by the late Dr. Mahaffy, provost of Trinity College, Dublin, it would seem that though a few asses had been used for their milk, and as sires for mules, the donkey as a beast of burden only came into general use in Ireland during the early part of the nineteenth century. Seeking for 'any large causes' to account for this in a country hitherto full of horses and ponies, he writes: 'It was obvious to think of the Peninsular War which lasted 1808–13, and to which the British Expedition actually started from Cork. The excellent index to that precious book, *Wellington's Despatches,* in twelve volumes (Gurwood), shows that he was in constant anxiety about his supply of horses. He even discusses whether it were practical to import them from America or from Brazil for his army. He spoke of £30 or £40 each, then a very large sum, being given for cavalry horses, and complains that England and Ireland seem unable to supply one-twentieth of the horses which the French can command. All this makes it perfectly certain that there must have been a great drain on Irish horses, not only those fit for cavalry, but cart horses, which Wellington tells us are unfit for that purpose, and lighter horses used for draught and transport. This depletion of the country as to horses must have given a singular advantage to those who offered the ass as a cheap and safe substitute, not liable to be bought at fancy prices for the war; and so by some silent process, probably by the poor and for the poor, this useful beast of burden came into Ireland almost surreptitiously till it spread over all the country. While the great Duke was conquering the Peninsula, the little ass was conquering Ireland. And, let me add, that a peaceful conquest is often more enduring than a brilliant one.'

Many stories are told of 'The Great Mahaffy.' Suffice it to say that it was he, a Doctor of Divinity, who first enunciated the 'biological' truth that 'an Irish Bull is always pregnant with humour.'

A mile from the head of the valley we are back by the lake, whose ripples echo the breathing of the winds. A golden moth across the water, a crimson dragon-fly from grass to grass, gnats in the halos of their sunlit wings.

'Elsewhere there are places made holy by man,
But Gougane was made holy by God.'

CHAPTER THIRTY-THREE

IN THE DISTRICT of Iveleary (*Uibh Laoghaire,* the descendants of Leary) surnames are few, and most people are
known either by the name of the place where they live, the
trade they pursue, or the Christian name of one of their
parents. My friend, Batty Leary, is known as Batty Kit
after his mother Kate. His son Timmy is Timmy Batt, and
Timmy's son, little Bartholomew, will be Batty Tim Batt
when he grows up. Connie Cronin of Gougane Barra is
Connie Gougane, Shawn Kelleher, the postman, is 'Shawn
the Post.'

This is a country peopled by more than many are aware.
'Fairies? The place is paved with them.' Ask Batty Kit
about the man who sat up alongside of him on the cart one
night, a little man in a white bawneen (homespun coat).

'I'm terrible tired,' said the little man.

'And where are you going?' asked Batty.

'I'm looking for a nurse,' said he, 'for one of our children. I must have a woman in, after childbirth,' said he.
'Last night I travelled seventeen miles, and no sooner did
I get to the house than a cock crowed and I was driven off.
And I went another fourteen miles, and as I got to the
house a hound bayed and I was driven off, and by that time
it was dawn. Now to-night I'm going east, to a woman be-

yond Inchinossig, and I must get her or our child will die.'
The little man stopped talking. The cart jogged on. After
a while Batty looked across to ask a question. But there
was no one beside him on the car. The little man had disappeared completely. And they were just passing the lane
that led up to Inchinossig.

Ask Patsy Kit about Shawn O'Reilly who used to be
going the roads selling fish. He will tell you how 'One
night Shawn tied his ass to a tree by the road and went up
to a cottage to redden his pipe, for he had no matches.
And they were having a dance inside, and there was a little
old woman by the fire. "Come in," said she. "Here's a fine
young girl wants a man to dance with her." And she was the
grandest girl ever, and the two of them danced jigs and
reels and sets all the night. And the piper was playing away
all the time. So, after the dance was over a man came round
with the hat to collect for the piper, and Shawn put four-
pence in the hat. He said good-bye to them then, and he
said he'd be coming again on his way back from the fair,
and he'd be sure to call in to see them. So they parted, the
greatest friends in the world. 'Twas a week later when
Shawn was travelling back over the same road, and he was
thinking to himself 'twould be nice to drop in for another
dance, that he came to the spot, or what he thought was
the spot, for divil a sign of the cottage. The longer he
looked the surer he was that he was in the right place, and
then he saw the droppings of the ass under the tree where
he had tied him, so that he was quite sure. Then what
did he see before him on a stone but his own four pennies,
and that was all he ever heard or saw of the cottage after.'

Con Jack Boflin will tell you how his father, and a friend
of his father's, were once taken by the fairies for a night.
'They didn't know it at the time, but the two of them were

in bed, sick, for a week after. And they wouldn't have known, either, what had happened to them if it hadn't been for an aunt of the father's. They both told her what they'd been dreaming, and 'twas the same dream the two of them had been dreaming. 'Twas playing football the two of them thought they'd been. And each of them thought he'd left behind a small little bit of a scarf he'd been given when he was playing. And when the old aunt went along, didn't she find the two little scarfs alongside of each other on the field where she was after being told.'

There was another man taken, too, for the night, to act as sponsor at a christening, and he couldn't rise out of his bed for a week after. 'Oh, yes, they had a priest. 'Twas Father Murphy who'd been dead three years.'

And at the lios, the fort, over in the townland of Cahir, lights are seen at night, but they are never there when one goes to find them, and the man who owns the farm put up a wire fence across the lios, and wasn't it taken down before the morning.

Shawn, the Post, told Connie Gougane that he thought I must be a 'broken-out missioner.' When I mentioned this to him he said: 'Oh, but you'd be the lovely man to hear a confession.' 'If I had your confession on paper,' I told him, 'I wouldn't need to write another book.'

On the day that I went over the hills with Shawn on his rounds, we had fifteen miles to travel, mostly over mountainy bog. We left his bicycle, his overcoat, and a bottle of brandy by the side of the road while we were away for most of the day. The brandy was for an old woman near his home who was sick. 'Safe, is it?' said he. 'Safe as in the bank in Cork. Safer, maybe. You couldn't tell what them fellows would be up to with a bottle.' For twenty years he had left things in that very spot and never was one of them touched.

A woman called out to us from a cottage: 'Haven't you a letter for me, Shawn?'

'What would you want a letter for?'

'From my husband.'

'And for what would he be writing to you?'

'To say when he's coming home.'

'Never fear. He won't surprise you. Before ever he's at the cross-roads he'll have his ears up and be neighing like a horse.'

We climbed some eight hundred feet up the mountain. With every step the heather grew softer, the wind stronger, the sheep wilder. Then we dropped into a cottage 'for a sit down.' No sooner had we arrived than the table was spread and a meal set before us. It was the same when we reached our destination.

'What day of the month is it?' asked the daughter of the house.

'It's the twelfth,' said Shawn.

'Faith, then, I'm two days older than I thought I was.'

'Faith, then, you don't look it,' said Shawn.

We sat in to the table. The daughter of the house brought in more turf. 'Some builds a fire you can pull up to but she builds one you must stand back from,' said Shawn.

Hospitality has ever been held in high esteem in Ireland, and nowhere more than in the south. At Dunisky, near to the Lee above Carrigadrohid, a Mr. Edward McSweeney had a stone set up at the approach to his house, inviting all passers-by to lodging and refreshment. It is said that a less generous member of that family who, at a later date, removed the stone never prospered after. During the fifteenth century the steward of Mogeely Castle, without his lord's permission, sent invitations to a number of the chiefs of Munster to spend a month at the castle. The invitations were accepted with alacrity, 'nor could the earl say them nay, though the castle was not overstocked with provisions.' All went well, however, until one day when the servants of the castle informed their master that his guests had eaten everything in the house, and that there was, literally, nothing for dinner. Here, indeed was a predicament. The honour of the earl and his house was at stake. In his hour of desperation he could think of one course alone by which he might escape his obligations. He organized a hunt. But before sallying forth he left instructions with his servants that they were to burn down the castle while he and his guests were absent. That same evening he returned with a sad and anxious heart to find the house still standing. Only was his mind set at rest when the steward drew him aside and explained that, during the day, he and the rest of the household had carried out a raid on the lands of their neighbours (among them probably those of some of their guests) and had taken 'a prey of corn and cattle which would sustain both castle and credit for months.'

CHAPTER THIRTY~FOUR

THERE ARE TWO HOTELS at Gougane, owned by two brothers, Connie and Denny Cronin. Connie is slightly larger than Denny, so his hotel has an extra room. There is a pair of gate-posts, but no gate, between the two buildings. They stand together beside the lake. Scarcely another house within miles. Only the mountains on every side.

Sometimes of an evening I sit in Connie's kitchen, sometimes I visit Denny's. In Connie's there is a modern range, and near to it will be sitting Grannie Cronin with the infant Margaret on her knee, while little Breda will be building houses of bricks or putting her dolls to bed. Jer, who helps with the sheep and the turf and the cows and the hay and the corn and the reclaiming of new pastures and everything else, and Michael, who helps Jer in all those same jobs, will be sitting around, and Mary and Nelly, who help Joan, Connie's wife, in the house, will be busy about the house, and Connie, the man of the house, will be talking to Dan Moore or Pattie Cronin or Timmy Batt, who have dropped in for a glass of stout, a story, or a song.

'Did you hear about Mike Joe Callaghan?' says Connie. 'They say he saw a woman who was dead a long while come up and go into his stable. When he went to look for her she wasn't there at all. But the horse died soon after. 'Twas as if she'd come to look for it.'

'Sure, my father,' says Nellie, whose full name is Nell Dan Mick Owen, 'was visiting one night with a friend of his, and they called at the house of another man whose wife was after dying. She'd left him with two young children. And while my father's friend was inside, asking the man would he come for a walk, my father saw the children's mother come up off the road, and look in the door at the two children, and then disappear into the hedge again.'

'And wasn't there an old man,' says Jer, 'beyond the Pass, who died a while ago, and he leaving a horse behind him. He left it to his nephew. And some time after he died the horse took sick. So the nephew called in a neighbour to see what he could do for the horse, and the two of them went down together into the stall. And there was the old man, and he standing by the horse, stroking its neck. And the horse died soon after.'

'And,' says Michael, 'there was another man died and left a horse behind him. 'Twas a horse that he was very fond of riding. And as often as ever the new owner went to the stable in the morning, he'd find the horse lathered with sweat, and the marks of the saddle and girth on him. And that with the stable door locked overnight.'

The best story teller that I have ever heard is Con Jack Borlin. Con can take the simplest child's fairy story like *The Forty Thieves* or *Jack and the Beanstalk* and tell it with as much conviction and such a wealth of circumstantial detail that any one listening, however sophisticated, will be carried away by the 'truth' of it. If he tells of *The Forty Thieves,* he will begin with the widow 'whose husband was after dying a twelvemonth.' He will tell how of her two sons 'the one of them was married to a lady, a rich Irish lady, and the other was married to a poor girl. I dunno was it a carpenter or a shoemaker her father was.

Which would you say it was, Jer?' 'I'd say he was a shoemaker,' says Jer. 'I think you're right,' says Con, ' 'twas a
shoemaker her father was. Anyway the fellow that married
her was very poor, too, and he'd be going every day to the
woods to draw sticks; himself and his ass and cart. 'Well,
·maybe it wasn't an ass. Would it be a mule or a jennet,
d'ye think, Jer?' ' 'Twould likely be a jennet,' says Jer.
'Well, he'd be going there, day after day, with the jennet
to gather sticks, and you wouldn't get much for sticks in
them days, not as much as you'd get now, maybe no more
than a few pence for a whole cart load.'

And so on, maybe an hour to tell the story.

If he was telling of *Jack and the Beanstalk*, he would ex-
plain what a poor sort of a fellow, 'stupid-like,' Jack was;
and how he and his mother had but the one cow between
them, 'I dunno was it a Kerry or a shorthorn,' and he would
go into great details about the beans, and the difference
between 'broad beans' and 'scarlet runners,' until when
Jack woke up in the morning, 'wasn't there the highest
fence you ever saw in your life. Yerra, man, you never saw
the like, 'twas higher than the sky. The top of it was lost
away in the clouds. . . . And what does Jack do but start
climbing it. Wasn't he the brave man? Begod, he was
plucky all right.'

After that anything that might happen to Jack would
seem reasonable and natural to his listeners.

In Denny's kitchen I would find himself and his wife
Nelly sitting over the big open fire with the red setter at
Denny's feet and a sheep dog under the settle. The gun
would be in the corner, and a couple of pig's cheeks hanging from the ceiling. Kathleen might be turning the
handle of a churn and Nora would be trying to get a jig
or a reel out of the wireless. Half a dozen or more of the

local boys and girls would be playing cards at the table. 'Put away them cards and we'll have a dance,' says Denny, or: 'Put away them cards and we'll have a story.'

Then the cards would be thrown aside, and if there was no music for a dance the chairs would be drawn up and somebody would begin. 'There was a man had to go to the fair at Bantry, and he was driving, west, through the pass of Keimaneigh late at night, and suddenly he saw on the road a woman, and she nearly under the wheel of his cart. He put out his hand, and he pushed her away from the wheel just in the nick of time. And, as he pushed her away, she looked up at him and he saw her face and 'twas a woman was thought to be dying in a cottage close by where the man was living. And he thought 'twas surely dead she was. And, when he got back from the fair, he told what he'd seen, and the very time he'd seen it. And she wasn't dead at all, but that was the very time she was after taking a turn for the better. And 'twas all on account of him pushing her away from under the wheel that she lived.'

Then someone would tell of Mickey Dan who heard that his sister was ill. 'And, as he was going to visit her, didn't he see her coming to meet him on the road, and, when he came up to her, she wasn't there at all. He was frightened out of his life and, when he got to her house, she was just after dying.'

But wasn't it in this very kitchen that a pair of kitchen tongs had been seen dancing around the floor by itself after they'd all gone to bed. 'Twas a pair that had been left to them by a friend, and 'twas one night it was seen what was happening when the house was very full and they had to put a man to sleep in the kitchen. And that was what made all the noise that they were often hearing.

'D'ye know Snave Bridge?' said Denny to me, one eve-

ning. 'You don't? Well, now, you go down from here to
Bantry, and the first bridge you meet is Carriganass Bridge.
That isn't it. And then you come to Pierson's Bridge, and
that isn't it, either. And then you come to Ballylickey
Bridge and at Ballylickey Bridge there's the fork of a road,
and the one road takes you to Bantry and the other road
goes to Glengariffe. Well, now, Snave Bridge is about two
miles beyond that, and 'twas there that Paddy Ruadh
lived.

'Paddy was a poor man. He lived in a cottage alongside
of the bridge, and three nights he dreamt that if he could
stand on Limerick Bridge at dawn he'd never see another
poor day again. So one morning he got up with the day,
and he never said a word to his wife, and it took him that
day and that night to go to Limerick, and he was there the
following morning with the day. And he walks up and
down on the bridge, up and down, and he sees no sign of a
bit of gold. And 'tis cold and 'tis wet, and he says to himself: "What the hell am I doing here?" he says. And then
he sees a man coming in with a load of hay, from outside of
Limerick. Four times that day this man came in with a load
of hay, and all the time Paddy was walking up and down or
standing on the bridge, the whole time. And when the
man with the hay was coming in for the fourth time he
stops and he talks to Paddy, and he says: "What in the wide
world are you doin' there?" And Paddy told him: "I'm
dreaming this long time," he said, "that if I was to be on
this bridge at dawn, I'd never see another poor day." And
the man said to him: "You foolish man," he said. "Haven't
I been dreaming, with a number of years, that if I was at
Snave Bridge on the road to Glengariffe, that, to the east of
the bridge, under a white-thorn-tree, there's a pot of gold."
And he asked: "Where are you a native of? Where do you

come from?'' he said. So Paddy said Bandon, which is a
different place altogether from Snave Bridge. 'Twould be
thirty miles between the two of them. Never a word more,
then, out of Paddy, but home he goes, and it took him the
same length of time, a day and a night, to arrive at Snave.
And his people were in bed, and he didn't call them at all,
but he goes out and he takes a fork and a shovel and he digs
down and he finds a pot of gold. Well, then, with all the
money, he bought a farm and a house and he was as rich
as you please for years, and when he had all his family
settled, he built a new house near the old one, and at
Christmas time he invited a party, and the school-teacher
was in the party, and the school-teacher says to him: "That's
a fine crock you've got there, Paddy," he says.

‘ "It is," says Paddy. "It's there a long while back," he
says.

‘ "There's writing in it," says the teacher.

‘ "Is there?" says Paddy.

‘ "There is, indeed," says the teacher.

‘ "And what is it?" says Paddy.

‘ " 'Tis in Latin," says the teacher.

‘ "Has it any meaning?" says Paddy.

‘ "Not much," says the teacher.

‘ "What is it?" says Paddy.

‘ "There's more below," says the teacher.

‘ "Yerra, that's nonsense," says Paddy.

‘ "It must be," says the teacher.

'But before ever the light was in the sky next morning
Paddy was below by the thorn bush and damned if he
didn't find another big pot underneath where he was after
finding the other. Sure, he's rich ever since.'

CHAPTER THIRTY~FIVE

THE STORY OF THE GOLD at Snave Bridge is of particular interest because, though there is as much likelihood that the story originated in west Cork as anywhere else, there are many variants of it, not only in Britain but on the continent of Europe. There is even a similar tale told in *The Arabian Nights.* The best known version in England comes from Swaffham in Norfolk. It tells of a pedlar of that town who dreams that if he went to London Bridge he would meet a man who would be the bearer of good news. He therefore goes to London, and, after waiting a while on the bridge, he is accosted by a shopkeeper who asks him what he is doing. The pedlar then tells of his dream. 'If I had cared for dreams,' says the shopkeeper, 'I'd long ago have gone to Swaffham, in Norfolk, where there's a pedlar living in a house with a back garden. There's a tree in that back garden and under that tree there's a pot full of money.' The pedlar, like the man from Snave Bridge, does not admit that he knows anything of his home country. But

he hurries back, and there, under the tree in his back garden, he finds the gold. Concealing the money elsewhere, he,
prudently, hides the pot among his oddments of brass and
other old metal. Time goes on, until one day a customer
looking over the pedlar's stock-in-trade picks out that particular pot. There is an inscription in the pot. What is it?
It's in Latin. Could he translate it? He could. It says that
'Underneath there's another twice as good.' The pedlar
pretends that such an inscription means nothing to him.
But he takes the first opportunity of digging, and there,
sure enough, he finds the second pot.

Carvings of the pedlar and his dog, some four hundred
and fifty years old, may still be seen on the desks of Swaffham church.

Another version comes from Yorkshire. Again it is London Bridge of which the man dreams of the story. Again
the stranger that he meets tells him of gold buried in his
own village. There are parallels, too, to be found in Scotland, France, Holland, Denmark, and Sicily. In Sicily the
legend has become attached to the noble family of Pigna-
telli, who even claim to be descended from the dreamer,
a seller of pickled tunny fish. He, like the heroes in the
other stories, had dreamed of a bridge. He had gone to the
bridge and he had been told of wealth that lay at his own
door. Returning to his home he had dug in the ground beneath where he had stored his barrels of tunny, and there
he found not only a 'magazine all full of golden money' but
jars and pots of other coin.

But, as might be expected, one of the most picturesque
versions comes from *The Arabian Nights*.

'It is related also, that a man of Baghdad was possessed
of ample riches and great wealth; but his wealth passed
away, and his state changed, and he became utterly desti-

tute, and could not obtain his sustenance save by laborious
exertion. And he slept one night, overwhelmed and op-
pressed, and saw in his sleep a person who said to him,
Verily thy fortune is in Cairo: therefore seek it and repair
to it. So he journeyed to Cairo; and when he arrived there,
the evening overtook him, and he slept in a mosque. Now
there was, adjacent to the mosque, a house; and as God
(whose name be exalted!) had decreed, a party of robbers
entered the mosque, and thence passed to that house; and
the people of the house, awaking at the disturbance occa-
sioned by the robbers, raised cries; whereupon the Walee
came to their aid with his followers, and the robbers fled.
The Walee then entered the mosque, and found the man
of Baghdad sleeping there: so he laid hold upon him, and
inflicted upon him a painful beating with mikra'ahs, until
he was at the point of death, and imprisoned him; and he
remained three days in the prison; after which, the Walee
caused him to be brought, and said to him, From what
country art thou? He answered, From Baghdad.—And
what affair, said the Walee, was the cause of thy coming to
Cairo? He answered, I saw in my sleep a person who said to
me Verily thy fortune is in Cairo: therefore repair to it.
And when I came to Cairo, I found the fortune of which
he told me to be those blows of the mikra'ahs that I have
received from thee.—And upon this the Walee laughed so
that his grinders appeared, and said to him, O thou of
little sense, I saw three times in my sleep a person who said
to me, Verily a house in Baghdad, in such a district, and of
such description hath in its court a garden, at the lower
end of which is a fountain, wherein is wealth of great
amount; therefore repair to it and take it. But I went not;
and thou, through the smallness of thy sense, hast journeyed from city to city on account of a thing thou hast seen

in sleep, when it was only an effect of confused dreams.—
Then he gave him some money, and said to him, Help thyself with this to return to thy city. So he took it and returned to Baghdad. Now the house which the Walee had
described, in Baghdad, was the house of that man, therefore when he arrived at his abode, he dug beneath the fountain, and behold abundant wealth. Thus God enriched and
sustained him, and this was a wonderful coincidence.'

It will be noticed that in each case the man dreams of
gold that is far away. 'Far cows have long horns.' In each
case he finds the wealth at his own door, by digging.

There is another tale that I was told at Gougane. It is
of an old man whose two sons were lazy and would not
work. 'Nothing that he could do would make them work.
Before he died he confided to them that there was a crock of
gold buried in one of their fields. He told them which field
it was. " 'Tis no more than a foot and a half below the sod,"
he said. "Dig, and you'll surely find it." After he died the
sons could hardly wait for him to be buried before they
began digging. Backwards and forwards across the field
they went, in deep furrows, for they were afraid to miss it.
But when they came to the last sod they hadn't found it.
And there was their fine grass field ruined, not a blade that
wasn't turned and buried. "What'll we do now?" said one
of them. "There's nothing we can do," said the other, "only
sow a few oats." So they sowed oats, and the money they
made was worth more than any crock of gold. And that's
how they learnt what comes of work.'

Some may feel that these simple parables of staying at
home to work instead of wandering afar in search of
'dream gold' may be of such a universal significance that
the wise men of many lands have, through centuries, produced the same sermon independently of each other. But

there will be others who believe that every folk-tale, every tradition, every superstition has its origin in some definite event, even if the links which connect the story, in its present form, to that event are no longer traceable. Be that as it may, there are few of these stories which do not point a moral. As one more instance, it is told that in olden times in Ireland there was a chief who owned a wonderful chain. If put around the neck of a guilty man it squeezed him to suffocation, but if put about the neck of an innocent person it expanded and fell to the ground. As a commentator has remarked, the links of this chain were probably close arguments and cross-questionings. We still use the phrase 'chain of evidence.'

CHAPTER THIRTY-SIX

EASTERLY WIND and a mottled sky, with a full moon breaking through. All day long the threshing machine had been at work on the farm across the lake. One could hear the 'chug-chug, chug-chug-chug' echoing again and again through the valley. By seven in the evening it had finished the work of five farms. Then it came to ours. In the haggard stood four stacks, one large and three small, the property of as many farmers.

'Would that be from half an acre?' I asked one of the owners, pointing to a small stack. 'Yerra, not one quarter,' he said. So small are the holdings in the valley.

It was nine o'clock, and dark, before the chaff began to fly, clouds of it like whirling nebulae of stars. The thresher was beside the largest rick. Men with pikes crossed and recrossed the lights cast from lanterns hanging on stakes. Ghostlike, the men moved in the deep shadows. Silhouetted against the moon, more men on the rick forked sheaves to others on the machine. Of these, two slashed at the bindings with carving knives, four fed the loosened sheaves into the trough. Three men stood by the sacks, at the shoots whence came the grain. Three more gathered the straw as it was voided, and built it into ricks. Only at midnight was the work completed.

That evening I had an invitation to a wedding party. It was to be held on the following day at a house about twelve miles over the hills. Wouldn't I come along with the boys and girls? Some of them would be walking, it was only nine miles by a short cut, but others would be travelling in a turf lorry. There would be a seat for me.

About five o'clock in the afternoon, next day, those who were to walk set out. The rest of us, in the lorry, didn't leave till much later. I sat in the front with Kathleen and Nora wedged between me and the driver. Through narrow lanes and over wild mountain tracks we drove. There were hairpin bends, stiff inclines, and stiffer declines. Young rabbits rushed here and there across the road. A donkey walking ahead of us on one of the hills stopped the engine three times. It grew dusk. In the lights of the car the fuchsia hedges glowed deep lilac. At the foot of the steepest hill the passengers who were in the back of the lorry got out. In front, I began to struggle with the same intention. 'Arrah, stay where you are,' said the driver. 'Don't move at all, Kathleen.' 'I couldn't move,' said Nora, who was between Kathleen and myself.

The engine roared and shot uphill. Round and round sharp bends we twisted. Up and up, steeper and steeper. 'They'll cross up the hill and meet us at the top,' said the driver. The engine stopped. 'They'll meet us at the bottom,' I thought, as we began to move backward.

The hand-brake wasn't working and the driver couldn't take his foot off the foot-brake. The door on my side had no handle by which I might open it. So, slowly, slowly, and then not quite so slowly, in black darkness we moved, stern first, down a narrow fenceless corkscrew road, a road in high repute among motor-cyclists for their trials.

We were saved by the weather. It had been too wet to

'cross up the hill.' Our passengers had followed us on the road. Now they stayed our course and built barricades of stones behind our wheels. So, by walking the last mile, we reached the wedding.

Through the open door we could see the crowded guests. Some were sitting on benches against the walls, others were dancing. The music was supplied by a man with a concertina who sat on the stairs. The light was from a single oil-lamp, but there was also a small red lamp below a shrine.

The bridegroom came to the door to meet us. He carried glasses and a bottle. It seemed to be the ritual that the glasses should overflow. Then we joined the party.

The dancing was mainly sets, square dances in which four, six, or eight couples alternate group patterns with jig or reel steps. Round and round they went, girls' hair flying, eyes sparkling, cheeks glowing, feet hardly touching the floor. After we had been in the house a short while the bridegroom came to where I was sitting and took me by the hand, leading me to an inner room where I was introduced to the bride and her mother, 'the woman of the house.' The bride and her sisters were serving a meal, in which I was invited to join. As each guest was satisfied he made way for another who, in his turn, was led to the table by our host. Dancing continued all the time. At intervals a double hornpipe or a solo jig, then again a set. Perspiration was pouring down the face of the musician. In spite of the crowd and its activity the atmosphere was as sweet as a meadow.

For the family of the house the day had started at five o'clock that morning when they had had to attend 'to the cows and all.' The marriage service had been at eight o'clock. During the later part of the day the bridal couple had gone for a drive. Dancing began on their return and would continue till dawn.

As the evening wore on seating became more crowded. Glasses were filled and filled again. The room got warmer and warmer. A little man on my left had a plump damsel on his knee. She overlapped on to me. On my other side was the fire, a big fire. Katie, whose hair is like autumn leaves in sunlight, was singing. The note at the end of each line was prolonged like the music of the pipes. She sang to the cadence of the spinning-wheel, a wheel moved by rhythmic touches of the hand. Her song told of a grandmother sitting by the fire 'drowsily knitting' while, 'close by the window, young Eileen is spinning.' The old woman thinks she hears a tapping at the window.

'"What's that noise that—I hear at—the window, I won-
    der?"
" 'Tis the little—birds chirping—the holly bush under."
"What makes you—be moving—and pushing—your
    stooleen
And singing—all wrong—that old *Song—of the Cuilin?"* '

   Chorus:
'Merri-ly, cheeri-ly; noiseless-ly whirr-ing
Swings the wheel, spins the wheel, while the foot's stir-
    ring;
Sprightly, and brightly, and airi-ly ringing
Thrills the sweet voice of the young maiden, sing-ing.'

Sweet, indeed the voice of the cuilin (*cuilin,* 'a maid with beautiful hair').

'Did you ever hear what took Adam his first walk?' asked Johnny McCarthy, who had come to stand beside me.

' 'Twas when he went to the Well of Paradise. And do you know when he did his first run? 'Twas when he saw the birds. And do you know when he gave his first smile? 'Twas when he saw Eve.'

'I'll tell you what it is,' said Paddy Mike Doolan. But the bride had come to lead me to another repast.

When, an hour before dawn, we said good-bye, two of those who had driven in the lorry with us elected to stay behind. They were not going to miss another hour of dancing for a mere walk of nine miles over the hills. As we drove home the eyes of a wildcat, a 'marten-cat,' glinted ahead of us. Later, a solitary horseman loomed out of the darkness. He was on his way to a fair at Dunmanway, fifteen miles away.

CHAPTER THIRTY-SEVEN

ONE NEEDN'T WAIT for a wedding to have a dance. In spring it is the season of Lent, but on summer evenings you will find groups of young people showing their steps in the open, on the concrete floors laid down for that purpose at cross-roads and such-like places. In autumn there are 'threshing dances,' as each farmer saves his harvest. In winter the long nights are reason enough, if reason is wanted.

But dances are not the only way of spending an evening in the mountains. There are few cottages that haven't their pack of cards. 'Twenty-five' and 'thirty-five' are the games most favoured. Sometimes the stakes are pennies, by which you may win or lose as much as a shilling in one night. Sometimes, especially towards Christmas, the evening's play becomes a tournament, with a prize that may be anything from a bicycle, unwanted by its owner, to a turkey or a donkey. It is a highly profitable method of disposing of property. As many as a hundred may gather to play. Each pays a shilling for his chance, and each may take several chances. One evening I went into partnership with Timmy Leary, and it was only 'by the purveyaunce of God,' as St. Brandon might have said, that I missed winning a buck-goat.

They were playing one evening in a cottage on the old road to Ballingeary. It was about nine o'clock and six men were sitting round the kitchen table. Over their heads pinned to a piece of Christmas holly was the prize, a ticket in the Irish Sweep. They played as three pairs of partners.

'What would you do, Jerry, if you won £10,000?' asked Connie Gougane, who had come with me.

'I'd stand the boys half a tierce of porter,' said Jerry.

'And then?'

'I'd lime the land.'

Jerry has a farm of sixty acres on the side of the hill. It is mostly bog. Even the best of his arable land is of a peaty nature. He has a constant fight against acidity in the soil. Lime and the want of lime is a subject ever present in his mind.

'What would you do, Shawn, if you won?'

'Begor, I suppose I'm too old to go round the world. Yerra, I'm not. 'Tis round the world I'd go.'

Shawn is seventy-nine, and still active and hearty. He never wore a pair of boots until he was fourteen years of age. Then he had to earn the money for them by working barefoot on the roads. His mother walked twenty-one miles to Macroom, and the same distance back again, to buy him those boots. In those days he often had no more than a few cold potatoes for his breakfast. A dish of Indian meal and buttermilk was a luxury.

'How would you spend the money, Mickey?'

'I'd buy a thousand cartridges.' Mickey is ever on the hills with his gun.

'And you, Johnny?'

'I'd build a little bit of a bridge over the stream,' said Johnny. The only approach to his house is by stepping-stones across a river.

Shawn and Jerry won the ticket. 'Are ye going to play it out or divide?' asked Connie.

'Yerra, divide, of course. Who wants all that money?'

'Twenty pounds would be enough for eyther of us if we got it,' said Jerry.

'Did you hear how Paddy Ryan, over beyond Coomhola, divided the gold he found?' asked Shawn, pulling up his chair to the fire. 'He was neighbour to Johnny Keohane, and Johnny had some wild heifers that would be breaking through everything. One night Paddy woke up, and 'twas a moonlight night too, and he after dreaming the heifers were in among his spuds. So he got up, and he dressed himself, and he went out, and he walked along to his field of spuds. But when he got there it wasn't the heifers that he saw in the field at all but two teams of men, and they playing football, up and down and over the rows of praties. Well, wasn't he in the state? "What in the name of God brought ye in here?" he said to one of them.

' "What's ailing ye at all?" said the man who was playing.

' "My spuds is ruined, and I'm ruined," said Paddy.

' "How are you ruined?" asked the man.

' "Sure, all I had in the world is in that field," said Paddy.

' "Yerra, man," said the other fellow, "go over to Christy Moriarty's at Bunane, and dig spuds for Christy, and you'll get more money there than ever you would out of here."

' 'Twas all very queer to Paddy, but what could he do only go back to bed. So next morning he got up and he dressed himself and he had his cup of tea and he crossed over the mountain, 'twould be near six miles he had to go, and he hired himself to Moriarty, and he began to dig the spuds. And there was a fine big house overlooking the field. "Tell me," said Paddy to the man alongside of him in the field, "tell me," he said, "who is it lives in the big house?

Isn't it the queer thing," he said, "that there's no smoke coming out of it?"

' "There's no smoke coming out of it, for there's no man living in it," he was told, "and no man has lived in it for years, and no man will sleep there even one night, not for all the money in the world. No man can sleep there and be alive in the morning."

' "Faith, then, I'd sleep there," said Paddy.

' "You would?" said they.

' "I would, indeed," said Paddy, "and for no money either."

' "What would you sleep for?" they asked.

' "All I'd ask in the world," said Paddy, "would be six clay pipes and they filled with baccy."

'So the owner of the house, Moriarty, the same man that owned the field of spuds, came to Paddy, and they opened the house, and they lit a fire, and they pulled up a chair, and they gave Paddy the half-dozen of pipes filled with baccy, and Paddy sat down by the fire and began to smoke. I can tell you, he was hardly alone when in comes a stranger and he sits down opposite to Paddy and pulls his chair up to the fire. But divil a word did he say. So Paddy went on smoking. But after a while he hands his pipe across to the stranger. And the stranger took it and for a while he smoked without saying a word. Then, all of a sudden, he up with his hand and he smashes the pipe down on the hearth, and it broke into twenty thousand pieces. But he said nothing, and Paddy said nothing. All that Paddy did was to take another pipe from his pocket, redden it at the fire, and start smoking. And after a while he passes it over to the stranger, and the stranger smokes it a while, and then, again, all of a sudden, throws it down on the hearth and smashes it to splinters. So Paddy lit the third pipe and the

very same thing happens again. And again with the fourth.
And no sooner had he smashed the fourth than the stranger
gets up and makes to the door. But Paddy is quicker and
he gets between him and the door. "What's wrong with
you?" he says. "What the divil is wrong with you?" he says.
"Is there anything I can do for you?" he says.

' "Don't touch me," says the stranger, "don't touch me
whatever you do."

' "I will not," said Paddy, "but tell me what's ailing
you."

' "I built this house," said the man, "and under that
stone outside the door I buried great treasure. Dig," he
said, "and give the half of what you find to my son, the
man that owns the field of spuds."

'So the next morning Paddy told the son, and the two of
them dug, and dug, and they found bags and bags of gold.

' "I don't want any of it. 'Tis all yours," said the son to
Paddy.

' "That wouldn't do," says Paddy. "Half to each was
what he said."

'So they divided it between them, and Paddy is rich ever
since.'

'Well, then, I know of two men who weren't so lucky,'
said Mickey. 'One of them dreamt of a pot of gold and he
and a friend of his went to look for it. And when they began to dig, a great howling wind, a kind of a blast, arose,
and as fast as they threw out earth with the shovel it was
blown back into the hole and into their eyes, and in the end
they ran away frightened. One of them was Taedy Mulcahy
who is now in Bantry.'

'Sure, 'twas his mother was leaving the fair at Bantry one
evening,' said Shawn, 'when a little woman comes up to
her and says: " 'Tis better for you buy half a dozen more

milk bowls," she says, "for the one on the dresser is very awkward for us to be drinking out of when we be a party." '

'It was,' says Mickey, 'and it was to her too that a woman appeared one day. "There's two things you must do for me," said the woman. "I promised a round at the well and I was never able to perform it. Go there and make it for me. And there's sixteen shillings instalment on my cloak. Pay it for me, and then I'll rest happy." '

'That's very different to what happened to my aunt,' said Jerry, 'her and the old woman living beside her. The old woman was talking about dying, always saying she'd be going soon. "Wouldn't you try to come back and tell us what it's like?" said my aunt to her one day. "I will," she said. "I'll do my best." 'Twas soon after that that she died. And one day, a while after they buried her, my aunt and her niece, Nelly MacCarthy, my first cousin, were going back to their farm after they'd been out for a bit, and they saw the old lady standing at their door. They were that frightened they couldn't go near her. When, in the end, they did go up to the house they found the cow and their two pigs were missing, and the roof gone off the calves' house. It took them two days to find the cow and four days to find the two pigs, and every time they put a roof on the calves' house it was thrown off again in the night, and they had to build a new shed before they could get a roof to stay on it.'

At this juncture in the evening's entertainment Denny Magrath arrived with his fiddle and Johnny Deasy with his flute. When, after midnight, Connie and I walked home over the lonely mountain we had forgotten all about fairies and the next world. Even so, 'twas curious the noise the wind made from time to time.

CHAPTER THIRTY-EIGHT

AT THE WEDDING in the mountains I had been invited
to Goleen. 'There'll be a welcome for you at McCormick's hotel,' I was told by the owner, who had had as much
difficulty in keeping his feet out of the way of the dancers as

I had. So one day I found a lorry going to the Mizen Head.
Goleen is a village about five miles to the north-east of the
Mizen. We didn't get there till one o'clock next morning
because there had been a few stops on the way. At each
stop there had been a delay. For instance, at one I met a
man who had been in the Munsters in the last war. 'I suppose you were an officer, colonel?' he inquired tactfully.
When it turned out that we had been in the same company
together in the Dardanelles there was occasion for considerable delay. At another stop, while it was still daylight, I
was watching some gulls in a ploughed field, waiting until
the driver had taken his orders from the village for bread,
buns, cakes, and flour. As I tood there an enormous police-
man came up to me.

'May I ask, sir, what part of the country you come from?'
he said.

'From Cork,' I answered.

'Faith, then, you're a fine block of a man and a credit to
it,' he said.

'Well, you've got about four inches to the good of me,
wherever you got it,' I told him.

'Don't say it, sir. Don't say it. Don't say such a thing at
all,' he said with emotion. 'I'd give half my size for an egg-
shell of brains. You've got them, sir, I could see, the way
you were looking at them birds. I looks at them too and I
watches the white light of the morning on their wings and
the red light of the evening on their breasts, but what are
they to me? Only gulls, gulls that come in from the ocean
to follow the plough. Tell me,' he said, 'a while ago you
were sitting on that bank beyond and you were thinking
and thinking. What was it, sir, you were thinking?'

'Was there a girl in a red dress passing along the road?'

'There was that.'

'I was thinking hadn't she the neat pair of ankles.'

'Wisha, my God, were you thinking that, too, the exact same as myself? And all the time I thought 'twas poetry was coursing in your head.'

'And 'twas only a girl's shins!'

'Don't they carry the future of the world?' he answered.

The road grew wilder, fields grew smaller, rocks and boulders increased in size and number. In the headlights we caught glimpses of swans on coal-dark lakes.

'There's a bit of a dance on to-night,' said Mr. McCormick next morning. 'Nora will take you along.' But, instead, it looked as if there was to be 'a bit of a death' so the dance was postponed. Actually, the patient recovered, so there wasn't even 'a bit of a wake.' But the dance was off and we sat in the hotel. I met Paddy Barry, whose uncle had been skipper of a schooner sailing between Wexford and the Continent. That uncle wanted no chronometer for navigation. He worked with an old alarm clock that had to be kept face down on the cabin table to make it go, yet he never missed his landfall. He had 'a sense of position.' Even in a fog, after beating backwards and forwards for three days, he'd know where he was. If he said: 'I think we'd be abreast of the Tuskar,' and the fog lifted, there they'd be and he couldn't even spell 'Tuskar.'

I met, too, Nicky, from the signal station, who could do as much with a pair of spoons as many a jazz drummer can manage with a complete outfit. And there was Jackie Sheehan, who never touched a drink but came in for cigarettes. All he wanted in life was books. He didn't care what they were about. He wanted to read 'everything.' The only book he possessed was an encyclopaedia. Every subject in it seemed good to him. And I was introduced to Peter

O'Neil, a retired light-keeper, a nephew of one Don Pedro Clavo who had risen to fame in Mexico. Don Pedro's real name had also been Peter O'Neil, but in Ireland Neil is pronounced Nail, and the Spanish for a nail is *clavo*. Hence when Peter arrived in Tampico his name soon became transformed. Unlike his uncle, Peter had never been farther from Ireland than a lightship. He knew them all and the lighthouses, too:

> 'Now we are passing the Fastnet Light,
> Old Head of Kinsale, it heaves in sight,
> Liverpool to-morrow night,
> And Jenny keeps the old place warm.'

That was a favourite chanty of the old-time sailors when homeward bound, he told me. To-day his hobbies are birds and wireless. He thinks of the one in terms of the other. 'D'you hear that sharp high-pitched whistle? That's puffins passing. Frequency note about 2,000. That cut-out is when they turn.' Shearwaters and razorbills, with the lower note of their wings, had a frequency about 1,000, while, he reckoned, the slow steady beat of the gannet was about 900. He said that when he was at the Mizen the puffins used to fly in V-formation until a peregrine took up its perch on one of the cliffs. When it saw the puffins rounding the headland it would shoot through a gully and strike two or three of them into the water, retrieving them later one at a time. After a while the puffins took to flying in a long-drawn line, far from the cliffs. Below his cottage there was a gully inhabited by foxes. To watch them, he said, you'd have to wait half an hour of an evening, lying flat behind a tussock of grass. Then when the dropping sun shone into the mouth of their burrow you'd see the tip of a snout appear, its nostrils dilating. After they had sniffed the air, two eyes would appear, shining like fire, and gradually the fox would push out its head and have a look around. If it saw nothing to cause alarm it would emerge further and still further until, when quite sure that all was safe, it would step out completely and roll in the sun. He said that the vixen had a number of earths, and that when her cubs were old enough she would lead them from one to the other, as it were showing them all available shelter. Then one day, while they were asleep, she would slink away and leave them to their own devices. Before that she would teach them to kill rabbits, bringing one back that she had nipped and cuffing them when they played with it instead of killing it. A fox's tongue, he said, would draw a thorn when all else had failed. He knew people who, whenever a fox was killed, would try to obtain the tongue. They would preserve it in spirit and, when required, apply it as a poultice. We spent an evening together on the cliffs watching the fulmars soaring, and a whale throwing its wisp of steam into the air. 'It's only a few years since the fulmars came here,' said Peter. 'Once on a time, less than a hundred years ago, their only nesting site in the British Isles was on Saint Kilda, but now they're all over the place. They nest on most of the coasts of Scotland and north England, and along down the west coast of Ireland, and, all the time they're prospecting, prospecting for new sites. Sometimes they'll visit a cliff and they'll sit there on the ledges as if they were brooding, and you'd swear they had eggs, but they haven't. They may be five or six years on a new site before they lay. One white egg they lay—just like the storm petrel or the fork-tail. You'd never think to look at the three birds that they are all the same family, the storm and the fork-tail so small and black and the fulmar as like as you please to a gull.

'Look at that fellow down on the shore. You could tell he was a landsman,' added Peter.

'How could you tell that?'

'Didn't you see him pick up the empty bottle and throw it into the sea? If a sailor picks one up he throws it inland.'

Because it came on to rain, and because one neighbour arrived with a fiddle and another with a concertina, I stayed in Peter's cottage for the night. Queer how the concertina and accordion have spread over the world since their simultaneous but independent invention in 1829, the concertina in England and the accordion in Austria. Ireland, the South Sea Islands, Spain, South America, many other countries, and every ship that sails the ocean know one variety or another of the 'to and from.'

Next morning I woke at dawn. On the horizon was the Fastnet Rock with its lighthouse silhouetted in the very arc of the rising sun. The sea was calm, scarcely a crinkle on its surface, and there wasn't a cloud in the sky. The great pyramid of rock with its beacon tower stood there in an effulgence of golden light.

CHAPTER THIRTY~NINE

A CAR WAS GOING to Bantry from Gougane. Would I like a lift? No, they wouldn't be coming back that day, but they could drop me on the road where it would be an easy walk home, 'not more than a few miles over the mountains.'

So off we went; through the pass of Keimaneigh, under the Deer's Leap, and along by the River Ouvane, until eventually they put me down.

' 'Tis only five miles across the mountains now,' they said, 'and you can't miss the way.'

Five miles! I must have been walking for five hours, struggling through long matted grass, climbing over rocks, manœuvring bogs. I saw the tracks of badgers where they had been rooting among ferns. A fox leaped from the heather at my feet, ran to a high cliff, looked back at me for a moment, and then disappeared through a crevice in the rocks. Coming somewhat suddenly over the crest of a hillock, I thought, for a moment, that I saw two small men disappear into the ground before me; indeed, I was positive I had seen them, yet there was no sign. Stories of fairy mounds and raths flashed into my mind.

'What the hell are you doing here?' asked a man at my shoulder.

(244)

'I'm trying to find my way back to Gougane Barra,' I answered.

'Gougane?' he said in surprise.

'It isn't very far, is it?' I asked.

'Very far? It's a good twenty miles, and you're walking straight from it.' I sat down on a rock to rest.

'And what are you doing at Gougane Barra?' he asked.

'Writing a book,' I said.

'Oh! 'Tis you, is it? Sure we know all about you. Wasn't Paddy Creedon over the other night, and he telling us how you and Timmy Leary were near winning the goat. Jerry,' he called, 'Jerry, come out, and Mikey, too.'

The two men emerged from where I had seen them disappear, and I was introduced.

'Whisper,' said the first speaker, whose name was Taedy. 'Whisper, would you like a drop?'

'I'd like anything,' I said, 'for I'm near dead with the walking.'

'Come in,' said Jerry.

From three sides of the landscape there wasn't the slightest suggestion of a cave, but on the fourth side, from which we now entered, it was surprisingly open. The roof was one huge flat slab of stone, heavily overgrown with moss and tufts of heather. It was supported in front by two large boulders, its back being deeply embedded in the rock. Any gaps at the sides had been filled in with sods of turf and heather. It was as natural a hiding-place as one could imagine. Inside, a fire had just been lit under a large three-legged pot that rested on two low walls of stones. I noticed that the wooden lid of the pot had been sealed along its edge, as if with putty; 'soap and linseed meal,' I was told. From a kind of hood on the lid a tapered copper pipe led to an angular coil. 'They're better angular, the angles

throw the steam from side to side.' This coil disappeared
into a barrel of water, but its nose protruded through a
hole near the bottom. Under the nose a stoneware gallon
jar stood, as if expectant. Flanking the barrel of water there
were two other barrels covered with sacks and flat stones.
One, at least, contained sprouting barley.

Mikey had gone out of the cave. He came back with a
bottle of clear white liquid, from which he half-filled a
china mug. 'Throw it back in you,' he said. 'Throw it back
in you.'

I did as I was told.

If I had swallowed a red-hot coal the effect could hardly
have been different. For a moment it seemed as if my toes
had come up to look at my face. Then a delicious glow of
warmth spread through my frame.

'Have another?' said Taedy.

'No,' I said. 'I must be getting on.'

'And how are you going?'

'There's no way but to walk, I suppose.'

'Isn't there Reardan's turf lorry going back to Macroom
at six o'clock?' said Mikey. 'There is,' said Taedy, 'and
he'll take you right to the cross.'

'Where will I find him?' I asked.

'Not a mile from here, and I'll take you down to the
road.'

So we sat back and I had another drop of 'the white
stuff,' and then I made a drawing of the still, and then we
all had another drop, and we sat and talked, putting an
extra bit of turf on the fire from time to time, and after a
while a gentle trickle began to flow from the nose of the
pipe.

'One more before you leave,' said Taedy.

'Put some water in it,' I begged.

Taedy took the cup out to the spring.

'I hope I haven't drowned it,' he said, bringing it back full.

There seemed little loss of strength. I have since suspected that clear water, but I managed it, and we started down the hill. All went well. There was a pleasant springiness in the turf, or in my legs, I couldn't be sure which. In no time at all we reached the road. We seemed to have timed things perfectly for, within a few minutes, the lorry appeared. In another few minutes I was sitting up alongside the driver.

'He'll drop you at the cross, and then you have only a mile to walk,' called Taedy as the lorry started.

I suppose it must have been the motion of the lorry that put me to sleep. The springs were not very good, and we were swaying from side to side. Besides, I had had a long day. Anyway, I fell asleep, and I was dreaming of an old man who had sat beside me in the bus from Inchigeela to Ballingeary, a few nights before. He was singing-drunk and he had wanted me to sing with him. Every now and again he would put his hand on my shoulder and say, in the most affectionate way: 'Sing with me. Why won't you sing with me?' Then he would launch forth again with:

'Red is the rose that in yonder garden grows
And fair is the lily of the vall-ey,'

the last syllable of 'valley' jumping up into a high note from which there was no recovery. He never got beyond those two lines. He sang them again and again, and ever and anon he would plaintively ask: 'Sing with me. Why won't you sing with me?' Of course, everybody in the bus was laughing at him, and, in my dream, I could hear the

laughter. Indeed, it was the realism of their laughter that
woke me up.

   The curious thing was that when I did wake up I wasn't
in the lorry any longer, but sitting on a chair in the hotel
kitchen with Connie and Joan and Mary and Jer and
Timmy all sitting round in roars of laughter, while I myself was doing my best to sing:

   'Red is the rose that in yonder garden grows.'

And for some reason I, too, could never get beyond that
high note in 'vall-ey.'

CHAPTER FORTY

Gentle reader, I do apologize for this extraordinary lapse, this accident, if I may call it so. I cannot understand for a moment how such a thing could have happened to me, me of all people. It is said that the country in which men dwell affects their character; that those who inhabit the mountains are of a different nature to those who dwell in the plains. I can only suppose that the sudden crevasses and treacherous bog holes that I had been negotiating must, in some way, have affected me.

It may have been just such an accident as this that dropped a friend of mine, almost literally, into the cave where he now dwells. I have not made tactless inquiries.

but I gather that there was some dispute with a landlord about the rent of a cottage. Twice within a year, my friend, on returning from work, found all his possessions dumped outside his cottage, and the door locked against him. The first time that it happened he knew how to open the door without a key, so he put his furniture back quietly and took little notice of the affront. But when a similar incident occurred again, and that within six months, it was, very naturally, more than he could tolerate. He therefore moved to a cave near by. When I say a cave, I really mean two caves not far apart, in one of which he sleeps, while in the other he spends the more contemplative parts of his day.

Now that his years entitle him to a pension this friend of mine is not quite so active or hot-headed as history suggests that he may have been in his youth. They say of him, to-day, that 'he is a pity, the poor fellow.' He would not understand this. Neighbours are good to him, so much so that when he speaks of anything that he may be doing, such as improvements to his dwelling, it is always 'we' who are doing it. 'We are building that bit of a wall,' or 'We will break away a bit more of that stone overhead.'

From living in such cramped quarters, and perhaps from wandering about at night when he is sleepless, his movements have become more like those of some creature of the woods than of the normal human being. His glances are quick. He is constantly watching, as it were always on guard. 'The fox must be busy to-day,' he says, as he sees some crows active above his cliff. He is suspicious of questions. His answers are indirect. You ask him if there are many rabbits about the place, and he replies that he often sees a weasel. It suggests, delicately, that he is not interested in rabbits; any diminution in their number must

be due to other causes. He once found a sheep, a ewe. It
had apparently got lost. He couldn't find its owner, so, to
get rid of the responsibility, he was forced to take it to
market. There was a ram, too, that he had found, much
about the same time, so he took the two of them together,
and he sold the pair for two pounds. Just when he had completed the bargain the owner of the ewe turned up and
actually claimed one pound as the value of his animal sold.
My friend had the greatest difficulty in persuading him
that his ewe had only fetched fifteen shillings. It was twenty-
five shillings for the ram that had brought the total up to
two pounds. And no sooner was that trouble over than the
owner of the ram must appear and make the same exorbi-
tant claim as the first owner. Again it took time to convince
him that his animal was not worth more than fifteen
shillings.

Between this cave-dwelling, a mile away, and Gougane
there live the famous tailor and his wife Ansty, short for
Anastasia. Lately a book about them was published. *The
Tailor and Ansty* it was called. Unfortunately, it was
banned in Ireland. I suppose the censors had never read
Chaucer. Sitting beside his fire on a wooden box which he
calls *Cornucopia,* by reason of its multitudinous contents,
the tailor will tell you that there have been no poets since
Homer. He means that the Tennysonian 'rectory lawn'
quality acquired by the muses in recent years has not been
entirely to their benefit. He will tell you that the first race-
horses in Ireland were got by taking mares down to the sea-
shore and leaving them there for the sea-horses to visit
them. 'That's how they got the speed of the sea.' He will
tell you that any man who marries a mermaid or a seal-
woman is ever after a poet. He will tell you that if you put
three drops from a raven's egg into a child's mouth before

it is baptized that child will know what a dog says when it barks, and he will tell you that 'the best way to keep a husband or a goose from wandering is not to clip his wings but to fatten him.' Meanwhile Ansty will be bustling in and out of the house, ever busy, yet never losing an opportunity of friendly banter.

'Ring-a-dora! Listen to the ould divil there in the shmoke, with his backside glued to the box like a statoo. Glory be! Always the lies and the carry on.'

One of the tailor's favourite themes for discourse is the difference between wisdom and learning. He says that a man who thinks he is educated because he has read books is like a man who thinks he is rich because he has money in the bank. 'Learning to-day has no style. It is like the clothes men wear, ready made. Many a man with a shelf of books in his head will travel the world and learn no more than another who goes no farther than his own hen-house. There isn't a man alive who couldn't see a new miracle every day of his life if he'd use the power of his brain.'

On all sides from the tailor's house gigantic rocks dominate the heather-covered landscape. Into their crevices holly-trees and rowans eat a way, and ferns luxuriate in the crannies. Over their surfaces crinkled lichens spread themselves like splashes of gold and silver paint, while ever in one's ears there is the sound of running water, a high-pitched note above the falls, a mellow murmur in the pool below. Up and down the river bed boulders are thrown, one on another, ever wearing, ever disintegrating, and the fine silt is carried to the sea to form rocks of the unimaginable future.

On all sides, too, there is human kindness beyond the telling. Often as I walked the roads and narrow lanes, not

only among those mountains but in the rich valley-lands
of the south and in the wild rocky country of the west, I
was reminded of that man of whom I wrote in *Coming
Down the Wye*. When asked his idea of happiness he had
replied: 'To be walking the roads of Ireland and to be
dropping coins into every poor man's fist.' Another man
that I met in County Cork said to me: 'The heart of Ireland is the heart of a woman. It will give everything in
response to love but yield little to force.' The heart of
Ireland is like its soil, rich, and soil is honest. What you
put into soil it will return to you, but you, also, must be
honest. When I went back to Ireland I wanted to return
at least some small token of what I had brought away in
youth. But it was I who became the richer. Where I
dropped silver I picked up gold.

CHAPTER FORTY~ONE

THE WEEKS since I reached Gougane had run into months and now the months began to look as though they might soon be a year. But the time was drawing near when I would have to say good-bye. We had had a party in

(254)

the hotel a few nights before I left, but on my last evening I sat with eight or nine others by the fire in Batty Kit's cottage. Some that were there were young, and some that were there were old. We did not talk of what was uppermost in our minds, that I was leaving next day; instead, the conversation ran on irrelevant subjects such as the east wind and the drying in it, fishing prospects, how many loads of stones a field might want for drainage, would Jackie Con marry Mary Tim?

Towards midnight I got up to go. The others rose, too. Batty Kit began to speak. 'I knew your grandfather,' he said, 'a hearty handsome man, and mad for the old stones and the antiquities; and I knew your mother before ever she was married, a lovely fine soft young girl she was; and I knew your aunts and I knew your uncles. We had the world of fun when they came out. Many the time I drove them, behind a pair of horses, twenty-one miles from Macroom, before ever there was a motor on the roads. Dick died young, God rest his soul, and John is dead since, God rest his soul, and your mother went, too, God rest her. And now I know your son. Four generations of you.' He took both my hands in his. 'Good-bye to you now,' he said, 'and may God Almighty watch over you wherever you go.' Then like a patriarch of old he threw his arms about my shoulders and kissed me. 'May the Lord God of Heaven love you,' he said.

And then I went out into the dark.

'Come here!' said Connie, next morning when I was saying good-bye. 'If ever anything happens to you and you want a home, come over and live here. But don't bring any money with you for you won't want it.'

'Come here!' said Denny, when I was giving him a last shake hands. 'Come back as soon as you can and I'll give you an acre of land over-right the river, and you can build away as grand a house as ever you like.'

Date Due

Demco 293-5